The Paradoxes of Interculturality

Offering a unique reading experience, this book examines the epistemologies of interculturality and explores potential routes to review and revisit the notion anew.

Grounded in different sociocultural, economic and political perspectives around the world, interculturality in education and research bears a paradoxical attribute of 'contradictions' and 'inconsistencies', making it a polysemous and flexible notion that has no definitive diagnosis and requires constant unthinking and rethinking. The author provides a toolbox of 'out-of-box ideas' in the form of fragmental yet standalone writings and follow-up questions concerning stereotypes about the very notion of interculturality and conceptual and methodological flaws in the way it is used. Readers are encouraged to critically reflect about interculturality as it stands today in global research and education. In identifying the paradoxes of interculturality and proposing alternative directions, the book stimulates a diversity of thoughts about the notion that goes beyond the 'West'.

The book will be an essential reading for scholars, students and educators interested in education philosophy, applied linguistics and the broad field of intercultural communication education.

Fred Dervin is Professor of Multicultural Education at the University of Helsinki (Finland). He specialises in intercultural communication education, the sociology of multiculturalism and international mobilities in education and has widely published in different languages on identity, interculturality and mobility/migration. Exploring the politics of interculturality within and beyond the 'canon' of intercultural communication education research has been one of Dervin's idée fixes in his works over the past 20 years. His recent publications with Routledge include the coedited volumes *Teaching Interculturality 'Otherwise'*, *Academic Experiences of International Students in Chinese Higher Education* and the coauthored title *Revitalizing Interculturality in Education: Chinese Minzu as a Companion*, etc.

New Perspectives on Teaching Interculturality
Series Editors:
Fred Dervin is *Professor of Multicultural Education at the University of Helsinki.*
Mei Yuan is *Associate Professor at the School of Education, Minzu University of China.*

About the Series

This book series publishes original and innovative single-authored and edited volumes contributing robust, new and genuinely global studies to the exciting field of research and practice of interculturality in education. The series aims to enrich the current objectives of 'doing' and teaching interculturality in the 21st century by problematizing Euro- and Western-centric perspectives and giving a voice to other original and under-explored approaches. The series promotes the search for different epistemologies, cutting-edge interdisciplinarity and the importance of reflexive and critical translation in teaching about this important notion. Finally, *New Perspectives on Teaching Interculturality* serves as a platform for dialogue amongst the global community of educators, researchers, and students.

Teaching Interculturality 'Otherwise'
Edited by Fred Dervin, Mei Yuan and Sude

The Paradoxes of Interculturality
A Toolbox of Out-of-the-box Ideas for Intercultural Communication Education
Fred Dervin

For a full list of titles in this series, visit www.routledge.com/New-Perspectives-on-Teaching-Interculturality/book-series/NPTI

The Paradoxes of Interculturality
A Toolbox of Out-of-the-box Ideas for Intercultural Communication Education

Fred Dervin

LONDON AND NEW YORK

First published 2023
by Routledge
4 Park Square, Milton Park, Abingdon, Oxon OX14 4RN

and by Routledge
605 Third Avenue, New York, NY 10158

Routledge is an imprint of the Taylor & Francis Group, an informa business

© 2023 Fred Dervin

The right of Fred Dervin to be identified as author of this work has been asserted in accordance with sections 77 and 78 of the Copyright, Designs and Patents Act 1988.

The Open Access version of this book, available at www.taylorfrancis.com, has been made available under a Creative Commons Attribution-Non Commercial-No Derivatives 4.0 license. Funded by University of Helsinki Library.

Trademark notice: Product or corporate names may be trademarks or registered trademarks, and are used only for identification and explanation without intent to infringe.

British Library Cataloguing-in-Publication Data
A catalogue record for this book is available from the British Library

Library of Congress Cataloging-in-Publication Data
Names: Dervin, Fred, 1974– author.
Title: The paradoxes of interculturality : a toolbox of out-of-the-box ideas for intercultural communication education / Fred Dervin.
Description: New York : Routledge, 2023. | Series: New perspectives on teaching interculturality | Includes bibliographical references and index.
Identifiers: LCCN 2022043457 (print) | LCCN 2022043458 (ebook) | ISBN 9781032442150 (Hardback) | ISBN 9781032442167 (Paperback) | ISBN 9781003371052 (eBook)
Subjects: LCSH: Intercultural communication in education. | Multicultural education.
Classification: LCC LC1099 .D4675 2023 (print) | LCC LC1099 (ebook) | DDC 370.117—dc23/eng/20221107
LC record available at https://lccn.loc.gov/2022043457
LC ebook record available at https://lccn.loc.gov/2022043458

ISBN: 978-1-032-44215-0 (hbk)
ISBN: 978-1-032-44216-7 (pbk)
ISBN: 978-1-003-37105-2 (ebk)

DOI: 10.4324/9781003371052

Contents

List of figures vi

1 Introduction 1

PART I
Becoming aware of the paradoxes of interculturality 19

2 The doxa of interculturality 21
3 Stances towards alternative knowledge 38
4 The Achilles' heels of interculturality 48

PART II
Dealing with paradoxes of interculturality 65

5 Towards a diversity of thoughts 67
6 Criticality (of criticality) 84
7 Unthink and rethink 98
8 Conclusion: Towards an approach to interculturality that is weaving itself ceaselessly 121

Appendix: List of terms proposed by the author 126
Index 131

Figures

7.1 The Möbius strip of unthinking and rethinking interculturality 99
8.1 Interculturality weaving itself ceaselessly 123

1 Introduction

What'll we do?

Just before writing this book I reread the text for the play *Waiting for Godot* by Samuel Beckett (1953/2011), which could not be more suitable for *The Paradoxes of Interculturality*. In the two-act tragicomedy, two vagabonds, Vladimir and Estragon, are waiting for a mysterious and enigmatic character called Godot. They are in the middle of nowhere, *waiting and waiting*. With nothing else to do, they often wonder if they should keep on waiting for him or just leave (Beckett, 2011, p. 57):

Estragon: What do we do now?
Vladimir: Wait for Godot.
Estragon: Ah! Silence.
Vladimir: This is awful!

Filling up their time, they suggest singing something, contradicting and asking questions of each other – *which all fail*. With humour the two tramps exclaim (Beckett, 2011, p. 32): "Vladimir: What is terrible is to have thought. Estragon: But did that ever happen to us?" They also jokingly consider suicide. At the end of each waiting day, a boy, who seems to pretend not to recognise them on each occasion, comes to tell them that Godot will not come but will appear the next day. *And they continue; they will come back and wait for him.*

Many commentators have seen signs of despair and nihilism in Beckett's play. However, the characters seem to be 'playing' to occupy their empty and meaningless existence: they play at waiting for someone who may not exist; they play at trying to entertain each other; they play at going through their daily routines and . . . they play at contemplating suicide. When *Waiting for Godot* premiered in Paris in 1953, many audience members felt discomfort at the apparent 'emptiness' and void of the two-hour play – which starts with the sentence "nothing to be done" (Beckett, 2011).

DOI: 10.4324/9781003371052-1
This chapter has been made available under a CC-BY-NC-ND 4.0 license.

2 Introduction

When asked about the meaning of the play, Beckett replied (1996, p. 136):

> I know no more about this play than someone who manages to read it attentively. I don't know in what mood I wrote it. I know no more about the characters than what they say, what they do and what happens to them. . . . I don't know who Godot is. I don't even know if he exists. And I don't know if they believe in him or not, the two who are waiting for him. . . . Estragon, Vladimir, Pozzo, Lucky, their time and their space I was able to get to know them a little only at a great distance from the need to understand. You may feel they owe you explanations. Let them manage it. Without me. They and I are through with each other.

Reading through the script of the play and what Beckett had to say about his inability to discuss the characters and the absence-presence of Godot, I could not help thinking about the notion that interests us in this book: *Interculturality*. Since the fateful year of 2020, which has seen (amongst others) a global pandemic, the death of millions of innocent people, economic devastation for the underprivileged, further racial injustice, (physical and psychological) wars, environmental catastrophes and polarisation of the world, I have (co-)written extensively about the notion, coming back to her[1] again and again. And although pre-2020, many books, articles, projects and educational initiatives materialised on topics of interculturality, I keep asking myself the very question that Vladimir and Estragon pose on many occasions: "What do we do now?/What'll we do?" *Should we continue? What is the point?* We all talk about this mysterious and enigmatic notion – INTERCULTURALITY; we all ask questions about her; we challenge each other about her; *we are all waiting for her* – and yet our world seems to be going out of control.

But like Beckett's characters, *we must go on. We come back every day, not as desperate beings but as beings who wish to strengthen their takes on this absent-present – although we will never be able to grasp her fully.*

The notion of interculturality (and its companions such as *multicultural, cross-cultural* or even *global*) has been part of the global educational research landscape for several decades now and is found in many subfields of education and beyond. As such, interculturality appears to be inevitable in everyday life as well as in research and education (Dervin, 2022). *She is not optional – and she has never been.*

I see at least three different and yet overlapping layers in the way we work on interculturality in research and education:

> Layer 3: 'Live' interculturality based on concrete interactions between people (e.g. an online conversation between someone from China and someone from Finland);

Layer 2: Representations and reports of interculturality (e.g. people describe and represent how they have experienced interculturality);
Layer 1: Interculturality as a subject of discourse (in daily life, in research and education; fantasised, theorised, ideologised . . .).

The boundaries between these layers (numbered from 3 to 1 rather than 1 to 3 to try to indicate a lack of hierarchy – an illusion?) are obviously fluid. In the book, I focus mostly on layer 1 (discourses of interculturality) but rarely on layers 2 and 3, although they often represent triggers for layer 1 in the chapters.

The book starts from the following argument: *Polysemic* and *unobvious* in nature since she relates to different economic-political, paradigmatic and linguistic perspectives, interculturality always deserves to be unthought and rethought so that we can enrich her as a subject of research and education and better understand (temporarily) what is happening to our world through different lenses. Interculturality is never analogical to any reality but to an uncountable number of realities. For Brecht (1986, p. 71): "When something seems 'the most obvious thing in the world' it means that any attempt to understand the world has been given up". Again: *We cannot give interculturality up.*

The paradoxes of interculturality in the book title suggest that there is not just one way of both defining and 'doing' interculturality in education and research but a large number of perspectives (some unknown), which makes it a potentially paradoxical notion – full of potential contradictions and inconsistencies. I also note another interesting entry point into paradoxes, linked to its etymology: *paradoxon* in Greek refers to the contrary of accepted opinions, of the *doxa* (common belief or popular opinion). Kierkegaard pushes us to explore the paradoxes of interculturality when he writes (1936, p. 29): "One must not think slightingly of the paradoxical . . . for the paradox is the source of the thinker's passion, and the thinker without a paradox is like a lover without feeling: a paltry mediocrity". Going back to *Waiting for Godot*, although the two characters have nothing to do, a life that is deprived of meaning and activities, they still hope for the (probably imaginary) Godot to arrive – *a paradox leading to passion*. The same goes for interculturality: we know that we don't know and that we will never know enough about her; we know that we cannot have control over her; we know that many assertions and ideas about her are illusionary and yet we are passionate about her . . . *waiting for interculturality.*

It is not a joke: interculturality as **politics**

A fire broke out backstage in a theatre. The clown came out to warn the public; they thought it was a joke and applauded. He repeated it; the acclaim was even greater. I think that's just how the world will come to an end: to general applause from wits who believe it's a joke.[2]

– Kierkegaard (2004, p. 49)

The last couple of years have pushed us to feel the world in more complex ways – not just 'think' it from a distance (Gramsci, 1985, p. 129). With the pandemic and the injustices that it has emphasised and increased, the wars and heightened tensions between world powers, interculturality has become even more concrete to us all. Although the other has always been *there*, now this same other is *with* us, as a friend, an ally, an enemy, a threat ... But what to do with the cries for help that we hear every day? What to do of the emergencies that we are facing? What to do with ... interculturality?

In a recent conversation with a colleague about our respective work, he argued (rightly, I thought) about intercultural competence that "there is no such concept". As we had been focusing on interculturality in our conversation, I added: "And maybe there is no such thing as interculturality ... it is not a joke". Silence ensued. *This marked the end of our discussion*. This was it. The end. *Why is it that we 'criticise' and even 'discard' (often rightly, I repeat) certain concepts and notions but still continue treating the idea of interculturality as if it were 'obvious', 'justified' and 'not to be disturbed'?*

The complexities of the world – of which we know so little and are uncertain of – are too abstract to be caged in a simplistic take on interculturality. When I questioned the very existence of interculturality in the aforementioned conversation, I was doing it in a somewhat provocative way to push us to think further, to see and think beyond the 'taken-for-granted', looking into interculturality 'oozing' in all directions – rather than 'transmitting' *robot-like*. The Italian artist Giorgio Morandi (cited by Barnard et al., 2007, p. 11) helps me clarify my thoughts when he says: "I believe that nothing can be more abstract ... than what we actually see. I also believe that there is nothing more surreal and nothing more abstract than reality". There is nothing more abstract (and surreal) than reality, than *interculturality*. What she is, what she entails and what she makes us do can be understood and problematised in so many different ways in different languages around the world that *waiting for her* (to hint back at Beckett) without real expectations or solid ideas is a stressful challenge.

In this book I argue that it is impossible to stop thinking about interculturality and that e.g. locking her up in a 'model' (which I compare to the fire in a theatre backstage) runs against her messages of complexities, her irrationalities and instabilities. I am not the only one to have warned against this and it has now become fashionable to do so, although a previous generation of scholars of interculturality in Europe had already criticised such 'penitentiary' tendencies (Zarate & Gohard-Radenkovic, 2004; I already made that point in Dervin, 2007).

The book is about epistemologies of interculturality, about different paths of knowledge constructed and produced about her. The very word *epistemology* is based on Greek: *epi* for over, near and *histasthai* for to stand. The book urges us to stand near and over our main character, interculturality, and to keep our distances from her as much as we can – to learn to extricate ourselves constantly from our views on the notion. *The book is not about summing her up.* Let's be clear about this: This would just be impossible considering her complexities; this is not a book about *a truth* but about *truths*. I have argued for years that we cannot deal with interculturality in a 'straight line'. She has no real beginning, no middle, and no end. Interculturality is a highly intricate and 'ungraspable' social phenomenon with unclear boundaries. She is also (un-)spoken in many tongues.

My point here is not to deliver homilies about her – although my calls for revising our views and takes on her could be considered as one! I ask a crowd of questions in the book, provide some (temporary) answers and urge you, the reader, to ask more questions and to consider different (provisional) answers, far away from applause and self-satisfaction. I am as critical as I can be of my own ideas, stances and silences in the book, going back again and again to some of the topics, revising my critiques and adding to them. I listen to my own ways of speaking in the book too and share my uncertainties and hesitations about the way I express my ideas. I tell you what I don't know, when I think I might be wrong; I share my fallibilities, my dreams, the results of my imagination; I also correct myself. In other words, I share with you these constant voices on my shoulders that keep telling me that I am not doing it right.

One important aspect of what is about to unfold relates to including politics and money in our discussions of interculturality – a topic that is very rarely taken into account directly and explicitly. I propose not to look at politics and issues of money as 'things' *out there* but to position them at the core of our discussions of interculturality and education. I am asking us to move away from the idea that the inclusion of this topic is *suspect* in research. In the special times that we have experienced since 2020, these two elements have dominated (often 'underground') our lives: Decisions about the pandemic were economically-politically driven (with many passing away in the 'West' because of such decisions); the current 'conflicts' between 'big' powers, which, through the (social) media, lead to 'common people' mistreating them, are based on economic-political competition and search for influence; the treatment of the 'other' in our societies derives directly from politics and money (e.g. foreign berry-pickers from Thailand and other places were allowed in Finland even when the country was officially closed; many became infected by the virus). While engaging with interculturality, we should bear in mind this couplet from a Chinese government official (Ming dynasty, 1368–1644): 风声雨声读书声声声入耳，家事国事天下事事事关心 (Fēngshēng yǔ shēng dúshū shēng shēng shēng rù'ěr, jiāshì guóshì tiānxià shì shì shì guānxīn), which can translate word for word as *the sound of wind and rain, the sound of reading, the family, the state and the world, be concerned about everything*. In other words: always be sensitive and alert to politics – not just 'knowledge'! At the same time, while focusing on the politics and economy of today for interculturality, we must be constantly reminded that our history of interculturality is neither innocent nor happy-go-lucky. And we must recognise the atrocities of the past and today, instead of merely embellishing the notion (Adichie, 2021). Decolonising is everywhere now and, little by little, the field of interculturality is speaking about it (R'boul, 2022). *Fair enough. High time.* However, decoloniality must not be hijacked and used as a 'trendy' and 'disenfranchising' tool for making us (still) feel comfortable. Colonialism is an unbearable and shameful form of interculturality. We must address the issue with honesty and modesty. . . . Listening to Kierkegaard's 'clown' very carefully.

A box of out-of-the-box ideas – (un-re-)thinking in fragments

One often gets a sense that interculturality is 'stable', 'grabbable' and 'analysable'; that one can pontificate her; that one can force one's own ideologies and fantasies about her on others 'naturally' (see Borghetti & Qin, 2022). When I write about her, I can pretend that I am in control of the notion, that I can possess her and that I can make her function the way I fantasise her to. But this is all an illusion. As soon as I step outside a book, an article, a lecture, she is more complex that I could ever imagine her through *my words*. In *A Room of One's Own*, Woolf (2015, p. 3) explains about a lecture that she was delivering on women and literature:

> I should never be able to fulfil what is, I understand, the first duty of a lecturer to hand you after an hour's discourse a nugget of pure truth to wrap up between the pages of your notebooks and keep on the mantelpiece for ever.

This book contains no 'nugget of pure truth' about interculturality.

Interculturality is an unstable subject that calls to be destabilised ad infinitum. That is why we need to take some time off to rethink, to stop misanalysing, mistreating interculturality.

As a whole the book can serve as *a toolbox* – a new kind of toolbox made of a *box of out-of-the-box ideas*. This box is meant to dig in and out of the complexities of interculturality, urging us to look at the notion through different lenses, bearing constantly in mind its unattainability and lack of uniformity. At the same time, stimulating our imagination in unthinking and rethinking the notion continually is another objective of this book (Camus, 1955/1991).

The book is constructed somewhat differently from other books on interculturality and requires the reader to navigate and explore it in a special way. The paradoxes of interculturality in research and education are reviewed in short written fragments in the book, based on what I have observed and noted in my engagement with the field in recent years. I am especially interested here in epistemological questions, i.e. the nature and limits of our knowledge of interculturality, examining its constitution, ground and presuppositions, as well as the tensions (paradoxes) behind her. The word *question* comes from the Latin *questio*, for investigation but also complaint/lament. This 'investigation' is embedded in my continuous efforts to help students, educators and other scholars enrich their critical and reflexive take on the important notion of interculturality. Although I do not provide single or simple answers to all the questions, I endeavour to make the reader think further and again about interculturality.

To avoid constructing interculturality as 'a pool of dead water', we should always consider her through the lenses of insiders-outsiders, coherences-contradictions, consistencies-inconsistencies and realities-imaginaries. As such, one assertion about interculturality can also be accompanied by a completely opposed one – cancelling out and revising the former, and, at times, back to the original assertion. We should also look at interculturality from an *either-or* position. A metaphor based on a work of art by Marcel Duchamp (1887–1968), entitled *Door: 11, rue Larrey* (1927), can also help us deepen our understanding of these assertions. The work is described as a "Three-dimensional pun: a door which is permanently opened and shut at the same time" (Schwarz, 1969, p. 496). Installed in a corner of a studio (90-degree angle), the door opens and closes the bathroom and the bedroom. Although two doors for two separate rooms would have been required, the installation allowed to close the door to the bedroom while opening the 'one' to the bathroom. If we go back to interculturality, while opening one of her doors, I am closing another one and so on and so forth. In the process, questions and answers pullulate and (at times) ramify infinitely.

The book differs from other books on interculturality and is meant to serve as a mirror for the reader. And while observing my struggles with the notion, sharing dialogues I have had, commenting on my own views and ideas, on others', revising them, adding to them, wishing to discard them, expressing my frustration/satisfaction, the reader can navigate for themselves the intricacies of interculturality. It is not so much about agreeing/disagreeing as about observing what happens when one examines interculturality through different (and at times contradictory) angles. It is also about trying to put oneself in other people's shoes when reflecting on the notion: *What would I write or say if I were a woman, a person from the Global South, a specialist from another subfield of research, someone who spoke other languages, someone who had different experiences of interculturality . . . ?*

I am aware that it is not an easy book to read since it does not 'go' in a straight line but takes you through endless labyrinths. *This is on purpose.* Interculturality is and should never be uncomplicated, and nor should writing and reading about her. In the chapters a constellation of thoughts is to be found. Sometimes I am critical of ideological 'orders' about interculturality (*do this, don't do that*) and, at other times, I give orders myself but ask you not to follow them. This creates confusion and feelings of alienation that are intended – working on interculturality should be *confusing*!

What about theory in all this? In Greek, *theoria* represents the action of observing, and of traveling to see the world. For Barthes (1985, p. 136), theory is the same as reflexivity. Theory should help us move forward but not 'embalm' what we do. A theory of interculturality needs to be as flexible and changeable as possible. A full theory of interculturality does not make sense as such, especially if it provides a framework to 'entrap' her. What we need is a metatheory which is changing, allowing us in the process to ask questions, to jump in and out of different places, to observe presuppositions, tensions, problematics. *Fragmenting and fragmented theory*. The way the book is written follows a principle that I have adopted for the past two years: writing in fragments. As such, the chapters composing the book contain chains of detachable fragments. A fragment can consist of short citations, aphorisms, anecdotes, notebook entries and pieces of conversation. Interestingly, the word *fragments* shares the same etymology with *fracture, fragile, fraction* (amongst others). From the Latin *frangere* – to break. This is why this book is not to be read from page one to the end. It is an 'orderless' book – like interculturality. It asks you to navigate through its pages aimlessly and to 'weave' ideas (the English word *text* is from Latin *texere*: to weave). I had this argument from Michaux (1997, p. x) in my head as I was putting the fragments together: "Books are boring to read. You can't move around in them as you wish. You are asked to follow. The trail is traced, one way". I wanted to liberate you from some of the impositions that a writer makes on his readers. This is meant to be a different reading experience, which corresponds to the unpredictability and randomness of interculturality. Open the book at any page, and land haphazardly on any fragment.

I argue that by adopting short fragments (from a few words to a paragraph), we can say more about interculturality, without limiting our thoughts, while pointing at the divisions in ourselves, others and between these entities. For Badiou (2017), a true idea must be one that divides and we must experience division while dealing with interculturality in research and education. Researching interculturality one needs to negotiate *multiple* identities, ideologies, words, theories, etc. By writing this book in the form of fragments, I change, and I do hope that you, the reader, can change too in dialogue with my thoughts and the ideas that I review and discuss. Let's follow Blanchot's (1992) suggestion that the reader and the writer should meet and walk together with the book.

Fragments also allow us to move back and forth, to sharpen our ideas, while revising and/or discarding them. Fragments are not dictated by a 'red thread' – although there will be encounters and overlaps between them. Through the fragments contained in this book I am like a factory worker whose machines change functions all the time so that the end product is never the same. *By their non-linearity and irregularity, fragments fluidify interculturality while liberating us from wishing to 'cage' interculturality into a closed system, from the law of closure that writing about her often urges us to adopt.* One cannot but treat interculturality in a fragmented way to reflect what it does to people. *To be faithful to its complexities.* For Deleuze and Guattari (1987, p. 492), fragments correspond to 'nomad art'.

By adopting the fragment format, I am also suggesting ways of what I have called (and developed with Jacobsson, see Dervin, 2021; Dervin & Jacobsson, 2022) *interculturalising interculturality* – or making interculturality a subject of research and education that we interculturalise, that interculturalises itself. I am hoping that this will serve as a leitmotiv as we navigate through the book. *The recursive loop of interculturalising interculturality.*

Each fragment composes the proposed toolbox of out-of-the-box ideas. Each of them was formulated in such a way that it is self-explanatory and 'stand-alone'. Together they describe the paradoxes of interculturality. Together they present a theory of interculturality that is unstable, changeable, recyclable, discardable. Together the fragments ask you to view her as an ever-changing character.

The way we speak and write about interculturality

> RIGHT, but how to begin, with what words? It doesn't matter, begin with the words: There, on the pond at the station. On the pond at the station? But this is wrong, a stylistic mistake, Cafeteria would inevitably correct it; one can only say a buffet or a newsstand is at the station, but not a pond, a pond can only be near the station. So call it a pond near the station, is that so important? (Sokolov, 2012, p. 11)
>
> I am rooted, but I flow. (Woolf, 1998, p. 83)

Working on interculturality is about othering and being othered *par excellence*. What I mean by this is that whenever we define her, attempt to explain what she does (or urges people to do) and what I consider to be 'good' ways of dealing with her, *I other myself, I other others*: I position my views on interculturality using certain terms and phrases to which I might give specific meanings or no meaning at all (at times). In the process I other the other – *I say what they don't say about her*. If I describe how the other sees interculturality (e.g. multicultural vs. intercultural education as monoliths; Chinese Minzu 'ethnic' education) I also other others' views on her. Language is power (Kramsch, 2020) and speaking for and over others about interculturality places them – willy-nilly – in a subaltern position, especially if I do not liaise with them. Researching and educating for interculturality should not be an act of decalcomania – transferring images and designs from paper onto a surface.

Since it is only through words that I can express myself about interculturality, I need to pay special attention to the terms that I use in my own language and other (global) languages to ensure that 1. I can give an opportunity to the other to get a sense of what I am trying to say, and 2. Allow for dialogues around what we/I say about interculturality. In my extensive work with Chinese colleagues, we have had umpteen conversations around words and phrases that we used to find 'obvious' (*but nothing is ever 'obvious'*) in our takes on interculturality. These conversations have opened up many interesting doors to un- and re-thinking interculturality. I share some of these conversations in the fragments.

Borrowing Iris Murdoch's definition of what a writer is, I would like us to remember that, while writing and speaking about interculturality, "In so far as I am also a psychologist, an amateur philosopher, a student of human affairs, I am so because these things are a part of being the kind of writer that I am". Writing is never innocent; it is an economic-political activity that does not always recognise itself as such – in the sense that it serves as a 'transmitter' of ideologies, 'orders' to do and think in specific ways (Roucek, 1944); writing requires using words whose meanings and 'flavours' our readers will have to decipher and (re-)negotiate for themselves and (often) for and with others. The words that we use to talk about interculturality are infused with unnoticed ideological takes, which have become automatisms to us – we repeat them 'robot-like' without asking questions. We use words and formulations such as (randomly) *culture, tolerance, community, citizenship, open-mindedness, respect, discarding cultural dross* (in China), which are polysemic (they can mean many different things to different people), often illusionary and, at times, empty. If we wish to move forward with the notion of interculturality, this is an issue that we need to put on the table constantly. This perspective is central to our criticality (of our own criticality, as we shall discuss) and reflexivity. It also plays an important role in theorising (again and again) the way we see interculturality. Every time we use a concept or a notion we need to stop and think: What does this really mean to myself, to the person who introduced it, to other scholars who have used it in my language(s) and other languages? This archaeological (looking into the 'origins' of concepts) and seismological (testing the movements and shaking around the concepts) work must push us to talk openly about the choices we make, how and why we make decisions to use (definitions of) concepts, why we choose a concept over another in a particular language. One of the best PhD dissertations I reviewed in my career was very special. Unlike most dissertations I had read, the researcher had written about the process of *change* in her work (how she had come to how her work looked at the end), rather than 'pretend' to showcase it in a 'neat' and 'ready' reformulated piece. She started her dissertation like any other thesis, and halfway through the introduction she stopped and started again, discussing how the 'nice' plans she had made at the beginning shifted again and again and led her to a completely different piece of work. *This was daring!* And although I know that many colleagues would disapprove of this dissertation, I gave it a top score for showing me how reflexivity and criticality of one's own criticality can function. Commenting on, deconstructing, discarding and replacing concepts, notions and theories were central in the dissertation too.

The fragments contained in this book aim to do the same, noting and problematising the ambiguity one might face in using certain words – away from my 'rootedness' towards 'flow' to refer back to the opening quote by Woolf. *Translatese* (see Dervin, 2022), this somewhat awkward way of trying to replicate closely another language, is discussed too (e.g. 'to cultivate intercultural talents'). The fragments also try to 'capture' temporarily the capriciousness of interculturality (which always escapes us) by proposing neologisms, new terms, often based on the combination of words ('portmanteau words'). I believe that language creativity can get us closer to the complexities of interculturality, removing some of the ideological flavours and automatisms found in rehearsed terms. Of course, this does not mean that neologisms are 'ideology-free'; on the contrary, but for a while they allow us to clear our mind a little, until we propose another term that might be (temporarily) more satisfactory. Some of the neologisms I propose (see full list at the end of the book) will probably sound 'clumsy', 'snobbish' and even 'ridiculous' to some readers. *Fair enough, it is just an 'exercise'.* I now believe that rehearsing, recycling and repeating the same words for interculturality multilingually, while believing that words are mere 'synonyms', put us in a 'routinesque' position that is often too comfortable. Borges (in

Alifano & Domec, 1984, p. 51) is of the opinion that "The dictionary is based on the hypothesis – obviously an unproven one – that languages are made up of equivalent synonyms." The use, overuse and abuse of the idea of decoloniality in English and other languages at the moment serves as a warning to me. *I must flow.*

Philosopher Gaston Bachelard (1994, p. 147) describes accurately what I am advocating with this book in this excerpt:

> Words are little houses, each with its cellar and garret. Common-sense lives on the ground floor, always ready to engage in 'foreign commerce' on the same level as the others, as the passers-by, who are never dreamers. To go upstairs in the word house, is to withdraw, step by step; while to go down to the cellar is to dream, it is losing oneself in the distant corridors of an obscure etymology, looking for treasures that cannot be found in words.

Although Bachelard speaks of poets here, as researchers and educators, we must explore the upstairs and downstairs of words as 'little houses', be curious of words and ways of expressing ourselves, renegotiating them with others in our own language(s) and others.

Navigating through the toolbox

The Paradoxes of Interculturality – A toolbox of out-of-the-box ideas for Intercultural Communication Education urges and supports readers to continue exploring the notion of interculturality by proposing a 'box of out-of-the-box ideas' for intercultural communication education. This book was written with diverse readers in mind and will be useful for researchers and educators with good knowledge of the field of intercultural communication education, who are looking for 'out-of-the-box ideas' about interculturality. As I stated earlier, the book is a *toolbox* which is not meant to be used as a mere *utensil*.

I am well aware that, beside the instabilities created by the fragments, your own meaning-making complexifies the reading experience of the book. In *The Hidden Girl and Other Stories*, Ken Liu (2021, p. ix) reminds us:

> As the author, I construct an artefact out of words, but the words are meaningless until they're animated by the consciousness of the reader. The story is co-told by the author and the reader, and every story is incomplete until a reader comes along and interprets it.

I used the metaphor of seismography earlier measuring and recording vibrations of the earth. This is how I see your role as 'co-teller' of this book.

I suggest that, as you proceed through the book (aimlessly or following chapter by chapter), you take notes on the following aspects (amongst others):

- *(my and others') 'orders'* to understand and 'do' interculturality (as well as their retractions and/or modifications);
- *bibliographic references* to other scholars and e.g. writers (agreement/disagreement/other);
- concrete *dialogues*;
- *contexts* (classroom, China, Finland . . .)
- *contradictions* and *inconsistencies* in what I say and make others utter;
- *inclusion of words and phrases* from languages other than English;
- *leitmotivs* (recurrences and reappearances of arguments, references, individuals);
- *new terms* (neologisms);
- references to *dogmas* ('-isms');
- what you consider to be *biases and stereotypes* in what I write.

When no example is given in the fragments to illustrate the points made, try to picture one for yourself. Once you feel you have explored the book partly or in full and/or returned to it a couple of times, go back to your notes and reflect on your feelings towards your observations, your own positions at moment X and Y in getting acquainted with the fragments. You might also want to reformulate some of the fragments in your own words, modifying them in the process. The fragment format fits perfectly this aim by allowing us to move back and forth, to revise some of our ideas and ways of thinking, and by (re-)considering some of the contradictions/inconsistencies that we might face when dealing with interculturality as a subject of research and education. I would also like you to ponder your aesthetic experience of reading the fragments when you go back to your notes.

All in all, the 'toolbox of out-of-the-box ideas' concept behind this book is original in the sense that it can be used as a way of interrogating one's own views, engagement and struggles with interculturality as a subject of research and education, as often as one can and as a source of inspiration to move forward (but without any single direction). As a notion that often divides researchers and educators, interculturality must be considered carefully and continuously beyond our own (often) limited way of engaging with her. Very few books available on the market, except maybe Holliday et al. (2021) and Dervin and colleagues (e.g. Dervin & Jacobsson, 2022), aim to train readers to reflect actively on what interculturality could mean and entail from diverse perspectives. And again: The book does not tell you how to 'do' interculturality in research and education but urges you to explore *again and again* your views on the notion, while being confronted by my ideas, in order to produce renewed knowledge about it.

The two sections that compose the book, subdivided into three subchapters each, help us first explore epistemological problems (e.g. common sense and myths about the notion, problematic ways of approaching her) and second, consider epistemological questions through e.g. criticality (of criticality) and a diversity of thoughts. The idea is not to establish a truth about interculturality but to describe it *from a distance*. Each chapter follows the same structure: 1. Definitions of the topic and chapter objectives, 2. A list of about 30 fragments (length of 10 to 100 words) organised by keywords alphabetically, 3. An *Interthinking* section with questions which I offer for us to 'dialogue' around the fragments.

Part I, *Becoming aware of the paradoxes of interculturality*, focuses on describing some paradoxes of interculturality as a subject of research and education. Chapter 2 revolves around the idea of the doxa. Doxa means 'opinion' and 'praise' in Greek. It has to do with common beliefs about an object of knowledge (Barthes, 1972) and is sometimes used as a synonym for *common sense knowledge, public opinion* and even *stereotype and myth*. The collected fragments in the chapter have to do with the ways interculturality is constructed as *doxa*, how she is worded stereotypically (e.g. the tautology of 'complex interculturality'), how she revolves around binaries (e.g. essentialist/non-essentialist) and how she can be manipulated as an ideology to promote specific political agendas (e.g. the current use of the phrase 'democratic culture' as a synonym in the European context). The reader is urged to become aware of and identify aspects of the doxa of interculturality in research and education, as a first step in questioning *ideological mimetism* and *clandestine a priori* (theirs and others'). The chapter called *Stances towards alternative knowledge* deals with the importance of reflecting on how we (are made to) treat alternative knowledge about interculturality in research and education. Over the past decade, there have been calls for *de-westernalising, de-centring, decolonising, de-essentialising, opening up our mind to other knowledge*, from within and outside the dominating sphere of the 'West'. Alternative knowledge refers to positions that question the epistemological hegemony of certain ideas about interculturality. The collected fragments help us reflect on the potential arrogance of looking down on or manipulating such knowledge; the importance to be 'genuinely' curious about other knowledge from different parts of the world in research but also fiction, philosophy and the arts. The need to emancipate from dominating voices and to give a chance to voices that do not have the power to speak globally is also problematised. With this chapter, the reader can explore their own curiosity in other knowledge and to evaluate their honesty in wishing to emancipate from dominating ideologies of interculturality. Chapter 4 reviews a number of shortcomings in the way knowledge about interculturality is constructed in research and education. The author uses the metaphor of *Achilles' heels* (vulnerable or weak spots) to do so and suggests, through the fragments in this chapter, to reflect critically on them so one might try to examine them in one's practices or (maybe) try to avert them. The topics covered in this chapter include (amongst others): the lack of interdisciplinarity, the use of the 'sloganesque' over the 'challenged', overconfidence in the way one deals with the notion with very specific and one-sided perspectives (and the fear of epistemological change that seems to go with them), consumption of knowledge over production, and giving orders over listening to others. After reading this chapter, the reader will be able to reflect on their own practices and those of e.g. the scholars they have engaged with, identifying some of these 'shortcomings' and starting to think about strategies to move away from them.

Part II has to do with dealing with the paradoxes of interculturality. While the first part is meant to guide the reader in observing and identifying some of the many and varied paradoxes of interculturality, this part asks questions that can guide them in moving forward with interculturality in research and education – without indicating a clear way out. As mentioned earlier, I have suggested that interculturality as a subject of research and education should be 'interculturalised' (Dervin, 2021; Dervin & Jacobsson, 2022). Interculturalising interculturality derives directly from the points made in Part I of the book: considering the complexities and range of paradigms, definitions and ideologies available around the world about interculturality, one should expand one's take on the notion and turn to a diversity of thoughts to do so. The fragments in Chapter 5 help us consider ethical issues in including a diversity of thoughts in our work, think of ways to do so, how to identify diverse thoughts about interculturality and how to treat a diversity of thoughts. All in all, the chapter introduces the reader to some form of 'prêt-à-partager' (Akinbiyi, 2011) as a stimulant for interculturality: e.g. to be ready to share, to listen to others, to ask questions, to be quiet and to look at oneself from a distance. Chapter 6, *Criticality (of criticality)*, serves as a complement to the previous chapter and revolves around the idea of criticality, especially the redundant argument of 'criticality of criticality'. Criticality is central in accessing and examining the paradoxes of interculturality, especially as far as epistemological issues are concerned. In most global research on the notion today, assertions of criticality are commonly made by scholars using perspectives such as *non-essentialism* and/or *decolonialism*. However, criticality should be critical of itself to be effective, especially when one deals with such a 'burning issue' as interculturality. As a notion that is anchored in the political and the economic, amongst others, a statement of criticality deserves itself to be evaluated critically to make it credible and valuable. This chapter supports the reader in being critical of criticality (their own and that of others), avoiding the problematic position of the Ouroboros snake who ends up eating its own tail. Many of the fragments found here evaluate claims of criticality and their relations to e.g. privilege and whiteness, and asks the question of what criticality of criticality could mean when it comes to interculturality as a subject of research and education. Finally, a certain number of biases, effects and illusions are discussed in some fragments as concrete tools for examining one's own criticality. Chapter 7 proposes to unthink and rethink. It represents, in a sense, a long synthesis of what to take away from all the previous chapters. Based on the two principles of unthinking and rethinking interculturality, the fragments used here focus on: issues of language in discussing interculturality (e.g. naming things), taking into account researchers' and educators' biographies and experiences in their work on the notion, working on interculturality so as to experience personal discomfort, making randomness a working principle in exploring ideas about interculturality, and accepting contradictions in the way interculturality is 'done' in research and education, corresponding to the complexities of the notion as a social phenomenon. The chapter aims to build up a habit of both unthinking and rethinking, following thinking and *ad infinitum* for the reader.

Before I let you explore the following chapters in the order of your choice, let me reflect a little further on my experience of putting this book together. First, once you get started with the fragments, you will notice that I have re-formulated them using *he/him(self)/his* instead of the original *I/me/my(self)* – this is the only change I made to the fragments that I wrote for approximately a year. Rereading them makes it a very special experience. *I know it is about me; I know these are my explorations of the notion.* But I now see the content of the fragments from a distance with this 'he', adding nicely to the necessarily feeling of alienation and *depaysement* that one should experience with interculturality. Second, although the fragments were written separately and are 'stand-alone', while putting them together in the chapters, I realised that they function 'spiral-like'. *This probably won't come as a surprise. Ideas do come back, get reformulated, reinforced, but also discarded and criticised.* Scholars rarely share about these processes and will tend to show the final 'end-product'. However, 'end-products' don't fare well with interculturality. Although the ideas contained in the fragments never end up being 'sharpened' in such a way that they are 'ready', these ideas allow us to 'rake' for more. The reader won't find any concrete recipe or answer to their questions about interculturality in the book. However, your mind will be urged to embark on an endless voyage of interculturality, like a nectar-gathering bee, flying from one flower to the other. When in need of inspiration (meaning: ideas you want to problematise further), open this book at any page and 'gather' critically and reflexively.

Notes

1 In the book I use 'she/her/hers' to refer to interculturality as I believe that she deserves to be personified. I use the feminine form as a contrast to my overly 'masculine' voice in the book. Often set in stone like a museum piece in research, I want to treat interculturality as a subject of research and education like a character in a novel, in reference to Deleuze and Guattari's (1991) discussion of concepts in philosophy and characters in a novel, who often serve as complex conceptual constructs. Interculturality is considered as a character in this book.
2 I cannot help but think here of George Bush's slip in his critique of the war in Ukraine in May 2022, saying *Iraq* instead *Ukraine*, at which many people in the audience laughed wholeheartedly. The amalgamated deaths of many innocent people in both Iraq and Ukraine (this terrible 'fire' backstage, to continue Kierkegaard's metaphor) represent an unbearable 'joke' for interculturalists.

References

Adichie, C. N. (2021). Keynote speech. *Humbolt Forum*. www.humboldtforum.org/en/programm/digitales-angebot/digital-en/keynote-spreech-by-chimamanda-adichie-32892/

Akinbiyi, A. (2011). *Pret-a-Partager: Transcultural exchange in art, fashion and sports*. Wien: Verlag Fur Moderne Kunst.

Alifano, R., & Domecq, B. (1984). *Twenty-four conversations with Borges: Including a selection of poems: Interviews, 1981–1983*. New York: Lascaux Publishers.

Bachelard, G. (1994). *Poetics of space*. Boston, MA: Beacon Press.

Badiou, A. (2017). *De l'idéologie à l'idée*. Paris: Mimesis.

Barnard, R., Daintry, N., & Twomey, C. (Eds.). (2007). *Breaking the mould: New approaches to ceramics*. London: Black Dog Press.

Barthes, R. (1972). *Mythologies*. New York: Hill and Wang.

Barthes, R. (1985). *The grain of the voice. Interviews 1965–1980*. New York: Hill & Wang.

Beckett, S. (1996). To Michel Polac (1952, June 24 and July 1). *The New Yorker*, p. 136.

Beckett, S. (2011). *Waiting for Godot*. New York: Groove Atlantic. (Original work published 1953)

Blanchot, M. (1992). *Infinite conversation*. Minneapolis, MN: University of Minnesota Press.

Borghetti, C., & Qin, X. (2022). Resources for intercultural learning in a non-essentialist perspective: An investigation of student and teacher perceptions in Chinese universities. *Language and Intercultural Communication*, 22(5), 599–614. https://doi.org/10.1080/14708477.2022.2105344

Brecht, B. (1986). *Brecht on theatre*. London: Eyre Methuen.

Camus, A. (1991). *The myth of Sisyphus and other essays*. New York: Vintage Books. (Original work published 1955)

Deleuze, G., & Guattari, F. (1987). *A thousand plateaus: Capitalism and schizophrenia*. Minneapolis, MN: University of Minnesota Press.

Deleuze, G., & Guattari, F. (1991). *Qu'est-ce que la philosophie?* Paris: Editions de Minuit.

Dervin, F. (2007). Évaluer l'interculturel: Problématiques et pistes de travail. In F. Dervin & E. Suomela-Salmi (Eds.), *Évaluer les compétences langagières et interculturelles dans l'enseignement supérieur* (pp. 95–122). Turku: Publications du département d'études françaises.

Dervin, F. (2021). *Critical and reflexive languaging in the construction of interculturality as an object of research and practice (19 April)*. Digital series of talks on plurilingualism and interculturality. Copenhagen: University of Copenhagen.

Dervin, F. (2022). *Interculturality in fragments: A reflexive approach*. Singapore: Springer.

Dervin, F., & Jacobsson, A. (2022). *Intercultural communication education. Broken realities and rebellious dreams*. London: Springer.

Gramsci, A. (1985). *Selections from cultural writings*. London: Lawrence and Wishart.

Holliday, A., Hyde, M., & Kullman, J. (2021). *Intercultural communication: An advanced resource book for students*. London: Routledge.

Kierkegaard, S. (1936). *Philosophical fragments: Or, a fragment of philosophy*. Princeton, NJ: Princeton University Press.

Kierkegaard, S. (2004). *Either/or: A fragment of life*. London: Penguin Books.

Kramsch, C. (2020). *Language as symbolic power*. Cambridge: Cambridge University Press.

Liu, K. (2021). *The hidden girl and other stories*. New York: Saga Press.

Michaux, H. (1997). *Darkness moves: An Henri Michaux anthology, 1927–1984*. Berkeley, CA: University of California Press.

R'boul, H. (2022). Epistemological plurality in intercultural communication knowledge. *Journal of Multicultural Discourses*, *17*, 173–188. https://doi.org/10.1080/17447143.2022.2069784

Roucek, J. S. (1944). A history of the concept of ideology. *Journal of the History of Ideas*, *5*(4), 479–488.

Schwarz, A. (1969). *The complete works of Marcel Duchamp*. New York: Thames and Hudson.

Sokolov, S. (2012). *A school for fools*. New York: New York Review Books.

Woolf, V. (1998). *The waves*. Oxford: Oxford University Press.

Woolf, V. (2015). *A room of one's own and three guineas*. Oxford: Oxford University Press.

Zarate, Z., & Gohard-Radenkovic, A. (Eds.). (2004). *La reconnaissance des compétences interculturelles: de la grille à la carte*. Paris: Didier Editions.

Part I
Becoming aware of the paradoxes of interculturality

2 The doxa of interculturality

This chapter could have been entitled the *mythologies* of interculturality or, simply *interculturologies*. I have decided to use the Greek word *doxa* – as a hint to the *paradoxes* from the title of the book – to problematise some of the misconstrued things – the 'goes without saying' – that one hears and says (unstably) about interculturality in some parts of the world. This is not meant to be a full catalogue of such assertions and statements but a snapshot of some of the doxa that retained my attention in the fragments (e.g. today's popular idea of non-essentialism to which I have also contributed in the field; see Holliday, 2011). As a reminder the word doxa (opinion but also praise) comes from the Greek *dokein* for *seem* and the Proto-Indo-European root *dek-* for *accept* and *take*. Amossy (2002) explains that doxa can be substituted by other words in the English language: *Cliché, commonplace, common-sense knowledge, public opinion, idée reçue, stereotype or verisimilitude*. For philosophers like Bergson (1907/1998), social beings have no choice but to approach reality as 'labels' to read. As a fluid, co-constructed but also highly economic-political construct in research and education, interculturality cannot but lead to the doxa taking over her. Just listen to discourses around you around interculturality: How much of what people say does not sound like a public opinion or a stereotype about the very notion? Claiming that performing interculturality requires openness, showing respect and tolerance corresponds to the doxa since all these terms, if not defined or positioned economically-politically and theoretically, will mean different things to different individuals. Think of openness to difference: how do you understand this 'order' and how do you translate it in other languages?

Before you start reading the following fragments, take a minute to list as many arguments about interculturality as you feel have to do with the doxa. Think of statements made in research, education or everyday life. Finally, try to explain for yourself why you would categorise them as doxa.

~ Fragments I ~

[Aura]

Interculturality as a word has a special aura ('energy'), flavour and quality. *Oh, how beautiful, cultures meeting each other!* Joy, happiness and happy colours. The aura forces us to experience her even before living her. But interculturality is not always a nice experience – at least not for every single person 'performing' her.

[(The) 'bad' essentialist]

The ideal of 'non-essentialism' (e.g. Ferri, 2018), whereby we are made to believe that we can approach interculturality in an apolitical and unbiased way, rationalises what he would call new hierarchies. *I am a good non-essentialist* (i.e. I am in control of my subconscious, my subjectivity, my take on others), *you are a bad essentialist* (i.e. taken over by imaginaries and irrationality). All categories essentialise *nolens volens*.

[Become]

"How intercultural have you *become*?" Does this make sense at all? As if there was an end point to 'becoming' intercultural. . . . One *always* becomes intercultural *together with* others (Abdallah-Pretceille, 2006).

[Benefits]

One often finds the idea that 'a culture' will win and benefit from the other *interculturally* in what many Chinese students seem to be saying about interculturality: *development, money* and *knowledge*. Are 'they' more honest than the rest of us? What is interculturality about in the end? What are the expected outcomes of the *inter-* and the *-ality* of the notion? The taboo question: *What present and future benefits for those involved?*

[Binary]

Interculturality is a binary; she is twofold. When we qualify something as *intercultural*, we assume that something else is 'non-intercultural'. *But is it so straightforward?* Considering the polysemy of the notion globally (she has more than one meaning and connotation), what we see as *intercultural* and '*non-intercultural*' opens up a complex continuum of possibilities and scenarios. We need to destabilise this dichotomy and ask those whom we classify as intercultural and non-intercultural for their opinions. He often gives the example of how students he had labelled conveniently as 'intercultural friends' for a past study questioned the label.

[Censorship]

Implicit/explicit censorship forces us to say things that we would not normally say about e.g. 'doing' interculturality in research and education.

[Complex]

No need to add the adjective 'complex' in front of interculturality. *It always is! Redundancy.*

[Copy-paste]

An impression of copy-paste at the beginning of some research papers on multicultural/intercultural teacher education: "increasing diversity represents a challenge for teachers". *Diversity* is never named (does it refer to 'migrants', 'minorities' and/or every one of us? See Wood, 2020).

[Cultural robots]

Someone claims that Chinese people help us understand 'the Chinese'. But do they even understand 'themselves'? Can a single Chinese represent a diverse population of 1.4 billion people (see Cheng, 2004)? What about a Finn, a Brazilian and a Cameroonian? Can they help us understand 'their' people? Interculturality reminds us all the time that we are not 'cultural robots' (see Wikan, 2001) and that sharing a passport does not make us 'clones' of each other.

[Democracy]

Why are we using fuddy-duddy words like *democracy* and *citizenship* when we speak of interculturality today in the European 'corner' of the world? Using democracy as a substitute for interculturality is a form of prevarication – a white lie, an evasion from 'truth'. He believes that the idea of 'European democratic culture' as a substitute for interculturality goes against democratisation of the notion itself.

By pushing its own Eurocentric agenda, such initiatives could close the door to alternatives. Should promoters of 'non-essentialism' and 'decolonising' in research and education still be tolerant of *global-, citizenship-* and *democracy-talk* in today's European intercultural-speak (this automatic way of speaking about interculturality, see Dervin, 2016; Robertson, 2021 on the OECD)?

[Dialogue]

The abuse of the word *dialogue* in times of crisis is disconcerting. Is dialogue really possible when the 'powerful' always seem to win? At a meeting about Chinese-European joint research on interculturality, someone from the Nordics lists amongst the staff they recruited for cooperating with Chinese scholars *a lawyer*. When asked if they hire a lawyer for their research with, for example, the US, they respond that there is no need for having one since "we can trust Americans" but not in 'dialogue' with the Chinese. The same person complains about the fact that Chinese scholars are very slow at responding to emails, being unaware that the social media app Wechat-Weixin is the most common way of communicating in China and that sending emails is becoming marginal in the Middle Kingdom. Finally, they are critical of having to write a report for the Chinese government for the funding that they had received for their research. He reminded them that when one obtains funds from the EU, one needs to write a report for the organisation too. While we call this 'transparency' and 'dissemination' in his 'corner' of the world, when it has to do with China, *it becomes suspicious*. How could one do 'joint' research without trust, eurocentrism and a lack of reflexivity and critical thinking (about e.g. peacekeeping projects see Minett et al., 2022)?

[Directions]

The word *interculturality* tends to force us to focus on *differences* and *clashes*. She pushes us in directions that do not necessarily correspond to our realities, which cannot but rely on the continuum of difference-similarity. A difference always relates to a similarity somewhere and vice versa. *Let's open our eyes!*

[Disguised whiteness]

He feels that *non-essentialism* is a new form of 'disguised whiteness'. We dictate what should be done and avoided in intercultural scholarship and education – e.g. *don't essentialise, don't use stereotypes!* This unattainable goal (one cannot *but* essentialise – even if just in one's head while performing openness) gives us power over the one who does not share this 'order'. *A potential fallacy used to (continue to) dominate the other, especially the one from the Global South – 'we' determine what you should do (see Dervin & Jacobsson, 2022)!*

[Distractions]

Non-culturalism and non-essentialism could be distractions meant to prevent discussions of what really matters: *those who speak are still the same privileged and powerful voices*. They also distract us from taking into account politics and questions of money in intercultural scholarship. In the meantime, the same dominating individuals accumulate *honours, citations, credits, fans, money . . .*

[Elitist]

Non-essentialism is an elitist notion that looks down upon the contradictions inherent to the social and the human. One minute we non-essentialise, the other we essentialise – openly or in a disguised manner. *The instabilities and inconsistencies of interculturality!*

[Era]

The abuse of the phrase 'our' era (as in *Our era of interculturality*): Is it really *ours*? Will the way people evaluate *this* era in the future as we see/define 'our era' today? 'Our' era is, was and will be *ours* and *theirs*. And the way they will discuss this 'intercultural' era might differ entirely from the way some of us see it today. He often has the impression that interculturality from the past is looked down upon – as if it was 'primitive', 'unserious' and 'simplistic'. However, in the 'past', there was no interculturality the way we fantasise her to be today (see e.g. Kalopissi-Verti & Foskolou, 2022 about Medieval Greece).

[Extremes]

Abandoning (or pretending to abandon, having the illusion that one can abandon) one set of propaganda for another one. *One extreme to another. Conservative* to *liberal* to *critical; essentialist* to *non-essentialist* – and sometimes back to start. It is never *either/or* but both sides of the same coin.

[Face-to-face]

Why do we need face-to-face contacts? Two years of online encounters have rendered the human more human than ever to him. The argument that 'there is nothing better than meeting face-to-face to make interculturality more intercultural' needs to be reconsidered and discussed more seriously. Being close to the other physically does not necessarily lead to 'real' interculturality (see Allport, 1954 and hundreds of papers questioning this assertion). One can be physically together, but mentally elsewhere. An obvious statement that we need to bear in mind.

[Fantasy]

Non-essentialism is a fantasy that still leads to hegemony. Its 'knowledge' dominates and leaves no space for alternatives. It still allows those in the centre, those who have the right to speak, to lead the way and to impose specific ways of seeing interculturality. Borghetti and Qin (2022), for instance, working together within the framework of an EU-sponsored project about interculturality 'sold' to the Chinese, observe resistance to this ideology amongst Chinese students who were introduced to it, ignoring the fact that linguistically, societally and ideologically (amongst others) the students might support (rightly) alternatives, have other interests concerning interculturality and might expect Chinese discourse instruments (see Yuan et al., 2022) to be systematically included as contrasting elements. It is also their right to reject 'Western' ideologemes ('slices' of ideologies) included in their project such as 'small cultures', 'translanguaging', 'cultural diversity' (what do they actually mean in China? How compatible are they with beliefs and ideologies of diversity and togetherness in the Middle Kingdom?). We are here on the verge of 'European' indoctrination and epistemic 'neo-colonialism'. Surprisingly, issues of Chinese Minzu education, which have to do with diversity from within, are completely ignored by the two scholars. *Non-essentialism fantasised as a 'Western' panacea.*

When everybody claims to decolonise everything then nothing is 'decolonisable' at the end of the day. Interculturality reminds us that we constantly falsify our claims on the world.

[Ghosts]

Ghosts haunting Finnish research on intercultural education today: *Ethnography, CDA, Intercultural competence, social justice* and *Bourdieu*. They are never justified, just included, *stated*. But they often sound unconvincing. *Why them and not other items?* Who pushes (novice and confirmed) scholars to insert them in their research?

[History]

'Making history' has become such a cliché of our times. How can we consider everything to be 'historical' today? How do we know that *it is*?
(see Augé, 2015).

Criticising English for 'colonising' European Language Education is diminishing the idea of *decolonising* – a slap in the face of those fighting against epistemological theft from the 'West' (e.g. R'boul, 2022).

Making statements about the history of the other to manipulate readers and trigger their sympathy for one's own (ideological) cause is unacceptable and condemnable in research. In a text written by a so-called 'decolonial' scholar, he reads that, in the past, 'the Chinese' were not eager to meet 'Europeans'. *But who are these people?* Who are we talking about? Whose history and interculturality are we depicting and, most importantly, for what purpose(s)? What does 'meet' mean in the past? Are we fantasising past encounters based on our own imaginaries? Why use an imagined voice from the past to create a new imaginary? Most importantly: What is the agenda of the scholar in question? *What is he really saying?*

Listening to French philosopher and sociologist Edgar Morin, who is over 100 years old, he feels invigorated. Morin has experienced all the major crises of the 20th century and reminds us that history tends to repeat itself (Morin, 2021). *An important lesson for anyone writing on interculturality.*

[Ideologies]

Each of us have clandestine *a priori* as far as interculturality is concerned.

"Why do they use the concept of 'race'? No one should publish papers using this concept in Europe". To which he is tempted to reply: "Why do they use the concept of 'democracy'? No one should publish papers using this concept in [add location of your choice]". Interculturality as *an economic-geopolitical Local Positional System (LPS)*.

It does not matter if one has a so-called intercultural background. It does not make them more intercultural or their research more diverse. What really matters in the end is what they do with ideologies of interculturality, how they deal with the notion.

We are not preprogrammed from birth. *Stop shaping our minds with frozen ideas about interculturality!*

Interculturality 'Otherwise' as a slogan. Who decides on the content of the 'otherwise'? (Dervin, 2023; R'boul, 2023).

A friend asks him for titles of books in which people define the perfidious concept of *culture* for her research on interculturality. He suggests not to pursue. *Culture is a thing of the past*. He asks her why she feels she needs to read such books and (more importantly) why she feels she needs the concept? She claims that everybody uses this concept and that she wants to know what they mean by it. He makes another suggestion: reflect on why people use the concept and why they have been made to believe that they need this 'modern-era' concept today (see Chemla & Fox Keller, 2017). (To the reader: *What do you do with this concept?*).

Two ideologically aligned scholars – one from a globally dominating space, the other from a 'minor' Western one – talking to each other about *multicultural education*:

"I am curious about your thoughts on this . . .
– I agree entirely with what you have said and written in your publications". *The end of dialogue. Ideological aerophagia* (swallowing too much air).

Reading what some of his students have written about interculturality, he sees a lot of automatisms. He can read and hear himself in what they say. *The unavoidable*. We might be brainwashed in our own language with others' ideologies.

Any statement on interculturality is ideological. *We are always ideological*. We think we know what is right and/or wrong about her.

Ideologies are ghosts that possess us. We don't know who hides behind them. Sometimes we name them ('liberal', 'essentialist', 'democratic') but ideologies do not exist by themselves. There is always *someone* in the background. If we can identify who they are – which we can't in most cases – we might then be able to deconstruct (and discard) these voices (see Althusser, 2020)! At the same time, we will construct new ideologies, once the former is 'discarded'. *Ad infinitum*.

We 'possess' ideologies. *Yes*. But ideologies also 'possess' us and force us to believe and act in certain ways. *We have agency, we say. Yes but* . . . Let's try to be strangers to the ideologies that we are comfortable with for a while, in order to try to move away from them.

Someone asks him how he defines intercultural*ism*. He tells them that he tries not to work on or from any doctrine or system.

After reading hundreds of articles about 'American critical multicultural education': There is a form of ethnocentric ideological positioning in scholarship of interculturality that needs pointing out and deconstructing. Too many of us are saying that we know what interculturality is (not) about and how we should (not) deal with it. *But can we be really sure?*

One project, one ideology. *One day: intercultural competence, the other: global citizenship.* Ideological mimetism. The *limited* Scheherazade syndrome: Rehearse, repeat without critiquing or changing. *Improvise as much as you can instead and continue telling different stories of interculturality!*

Copying-pasting ideologically-economically-politically informed 'scientific' frameworks onto other contexts, without questioning them, without admitting their lack of correspondence, will always harm the basis of research: *The participants*. We end up judging them with 'alien' ideologies (see Borghetti & Qin, 2022; Humphreys, 2021). He wonders how participants would react if they knew that they would be 'dealt with' by means of frameworks they would probably disagree with.

What he suggests is that we accept that there are different ideologies about and for interculturality across the world. The idea is not to create a competitive market of ideas ('the best wins') but to trigger dialogue for 'never-ending' change. It is not about substituting an idea with another but to *interculturalise interculturality* (Dervin, 2021; Dervin & Jacobsson, 2022).

[Illusion]

> Someone asks him what he thinks of *assessing intercultural competence*. He replies: "Would you assess humans for their humanity"?

Non-essentialism is an illusion. The illusion and disappointment of the bulldozer of non-essentialism which forces us ruthlessly to pretend to not be *humans*. The awareness of our humanity – i.e. we (re-)categorise and (re-)judge – is a certainty.

[Justice]

> "The idea of *social justice education* is more direct than *multicultural education*", says one of his interlocutors. Is it? What justice does *social justice* concretely refer to? Justice by whom and for whom and for what/whose purpose(s)? What is 'social' here?

[Listener]

> Seen in a scholar's bio: *He is a speaker*. Is that a 'job', a 'title'? *We are all speakers*. He wishes he could include in his own biodata *listener* and/or *observer*.

[Love]

> Love your neighbour like yourself. *What if he doesn't love himself?*

[Medical diagnoses]

He often wonders if the research participants whom we judge to be essentialist or culturalist would feel offended by we researchers judging them or if they would feel that we give them 'medical diagnoses'.

[Merge]

Absurd statement *par excellence*, considering the history of the world: "Different cultures should meet but not merge". Our history is that of *mixing, mélange*, and *mergers* – for better or worse (see Pieterse, 2020)! This statement is a good example of trying to stop the 'out of control-ness' of life and . . . interculturality.

[Miscommunication]

We may have the ability to *mis-* and *non-communicate* in seven different languages. The number of languages in one's head does not make us immune to miscommunication or mis-connotation. At the end of the day it is the co-presence of others that guides us through (mis-/non-) communication – not languages as such.

[Missing]

Why is missing a place, a country often perceived as *a bad thing* in interculturality – as if admitting *defeat*? Would you be judged for missing someone you love? He doesn't miss Finland and/or 'Europe' when he is away. He misses people; he does not miss them. He carries them with him all the time.

[Mother tongue]

The illusion of the 'mother tongue' as transparent and prone to 'perfect' communication. Not having the opportunity to 'taste' other forms of languages, even within their own, seems to blind 'mother tonguers' (see the 'postmonolingual condition' by Yildiz, 2013).

[Mutilated thoughts]

"*THE* intercultural approach". Is there such a thing? So many mutilated thoughts in research and education on interculturality. Why does he often feel that he is holding a half toothless broken comb that he has just dropped when he reads some research on interculturality today?

[Myths]

Someone suggests that critical thinking is about one being able to think *independently*. But can we think without others? The other is always there, even when we think that they are not.

The ready-to-speak of interculturality is alarming. When one declares something as intercultural, there is a danger that it might implode from within and die. He has also contributed to creating mythologies of interculturality through his work. His 2016 book is full of myths (Dervin, 2016)! And he will surely continue for years to come.

[Neurodiverse]

The term *neurodiversity* being used to refer to certain people with special needs makes him think: Aren't we all 'neurodiverse'? Don't we all think and learn in different ways? *Diverse* always seems to refer to the other, never to self.

[Non-essentialism]

He argues that essentialism is re-activated through non-essentialism. Claims of non-essentialism can represent an arrogant form of *atavism* – it forces us back to solidity, to solidify the other as 'condemnable' for not playing the unrealistic game of non-essentialism as put forward by some 'Western' researchers. One cannot *but be* fluid and yet fluidity does not mean that things flow gently and obstacle-free. Essentialism represents inevitable and necessary obstacles on the way to the other – and to self.

Non-essentialism puts an end to research. What could be possible after the end of the human? Nietzsche (1989, p. 90): "everything with absolute belongs to pathology". The current promotion of non-essentialism, blocking the way (unfairly and unrealistically) to alternatives, is pathological. In golf, when a ball obstructs one's line of play, it is referred to as *stymieing the game*. Discourses of non-essentialism currently stymie and confuse interculturality.

Overdose of non-essentialism. Misguided idealism. Non-essentialism as a gimmick: *We can solve interculturality*. But 1. What there is to solve will be different for the thousands of researchers and educators interested in interculturality, and 2. Where do we go from non-essentialism?

He is worried about how the essentialisation of some ways of engaging with interculturality in certain parts of the world systematically closes the door to people whom we need in order to disrupt our own ways of thinking.

Closing such doors also makes us too certain of our own ideological takes on the notion and leads to ideological inbreeding about interculturality.

[Obvious]

The use of the word *intercultural* seems obvious. It makes the object it refers to *obvious*. However, nothing is evident when it comes to interculturality. Interculturality is the enemy of the obvious.

[(The) other's shoes]

Putting oneself in the other's shoes is impossible. If there is one place to fill, it is one's own. *I must put myself in my own shoes* or – at least – wear one of my shoes and one of the other's.

[Passion]

He heard someone tell other interculturalists while sharing their contacts to 'stay in touch': "We share the same passion and vision". But during their meeting, no one explained what they meant by interculturality or what they want from her in terms of research and education or e.g. what upset them about her. As if by filling in one's contact list, one 'interculturalises'. *The empty subject thrown around.*

[Positive]

During a lecture, someone asks him to be 'more positive' about interculturality. "I would expect more positive views about interculturality here", they utter. What does *positive* mean here? Was the comment an indication that they disagreed with him and/or that they felt uncomfortable at the realities that he was describing? Is working on interculturality meant to be (always) positive/optimistic (whatever this might mean) or should it be closer to the world we live in today, where the way we do interculturality is increasingly worrying (wars, conflicts, 'money skirmishes', provocations, othering, media/ideological manipulation, etc.)? In the end, he did not consider what he was saying to be 'negative'. *Positive* or *negative* or *something else* are always viewpoints and need to be opened up . . .

[Properly]

In the end, can someone determine or say if another person does interculturality *properly* or *well*? No. He can't even tell if he is doing it 'well' himself since he knows that others do not necessarily share the same ideologies about the notion (*success, failure* as unstable subjects).

[Receiving]

The French phrase *idées reçues* translates in English as *popular beliefs, misconceptions, preconceived ideas, conventional wisdom, stereotypes* – or even *doxa*. The word *reçues* in French means *received*. Stereotypes are ideas that we have received from others (Barthes, 1972). Hence the need to do an archaeology of how such ideas are passed from one person to another – not to confirm their 'truth' or 'invalidity' but to observe their trajectories and what they tell us about *us*.

[Ritornellos]

The cliché of *good intentions are not enough* about intercultural/multicultural education has become a tedious ritornello – an originally interesting tune that is now played too much!

[Superhuman]

Someone lists *open-mindedness, respect* and *empathy* as characteristics that teachers must 'possess' to teach interculturality. *Does this mean that teachers are not humans?* In a similar vein: *We don't want our students to essentialise* could mean that we don't want our students to be human beings; we want them to perform being *non-humans*.

Non-essentialism essentialises the human as *superhuman*.

[Things]

What place do objects and things have in interculturality? How do they influence what we do together? Why are they always absent from research and education? Why aren't we prepared to 'meet' (through) objects? Things mediate our encounters; let's include them in our work (Itkonen & Dervin, 2017; Dervin & Yuan, 2023).

[Tribes]

Congratulating and complementing each other within an academic 'tribe' working on interculturality, without any critique, discussion or debate sends a wrong signal. *One should demolish each other's work in a tribe.* Destruction from within is a necessity to avoid *sloganism, too much comfort* and thus *uselessness. Destruction feeds moving forward.*

When we celebrate publishing a new article, chapter or book about interculturality, let's celebrate their flaws too. What has changed since I wrote it – which could be several years ago? What would I like to change about it? Working on interculturality requires to think in the future constantly. Unfortunately, today's obsession with 'selling', 'promoting' and even 'marketing' self and research blinds us in front of these important aspects.

[Trick]

Trans- or *inter-cultural* (Baker, 2022)? A trick to divert our attention? It is not the label that matters but what the terms entail and especially how to make them be *re-voiced* by the voiceless, by those who don't have the 'right' so speak about the notions.

[Triumph]

Triumphalism should be avoided in research on interculturality (self-congratulation noted in some research articles, such as 'my course helped the students acquire intercultural competence'). We just need to step outside our ivory tower to watch the world collapse today. . . . *Interculturality will never be triumphant.* And before he is accused of being overly pessimistic, he adds that this represents an extra motivation to continue working on the notion.

[Unbalanced]

The idea of 'unbalanced' interculturality makes no sense. Interculturality always is destabilised!

[Viruses]

– *Isms* and *non-isms*, such as essentialism/non-essentialism and culturalism/non-culturalism, are potential viruses that will end up contaminating us all. They feed on us as much as we feed on and profit from them. At the end of the day, it is not viruses that he is afraid of, but of we humans and of the truths that these viruses reveal about us. We spread these viruses, these doxic elements, we lie about them, we manipulate them, we belittle them, we use them as excuses.

~ Interthinking ~

Start by choosing two fragments from this chapter (like one you agree with; another one you find puzzling). Try to understand why you feel the way you do about these fragments: *What does make you feel e.g. uncomfortable and/or satisfied?* Did you identify other aspects of what I describe as doxa in what I write in the fragments? What is the 'power' of language in guiding your feelings here? What would you change about these fragments to modify your feelings toward the ideas they contain?

Now consider the following questions:

+ What comes to mind when you hear the word *intercultural* in English? What stereotypes about who we are as *people*? What emotions? Whose names? What objects? What 'orders' (what to do?)?
+ Who are your 'heroes' and your 'models' in the field of intercultural communication education? What would you want to ask them if you could meet them? What critique(s) of their work would you want to put to them?
+ When was the last time someone criticised you for doing something 'wrong' interculturally? What was it about? What impact did it have on your behaviour and way of thinking?
+ What is your favourite and least preferred *-ism* in intercultural research and education (e.g. orientalism)? Explain why and try to think 'otherwise' about them.
+ Do you feel uncomfortable with the idea that 'money' should be discussed as far as interculturality is concerned? In research and education? Think of your last 'intercultural encounters'; did it seem to matter?
+ How often do you say things about interculturality that you do not actually believe in? Think of something you claimed about the notion in class or in your writing: Were you convinced of your own argument, use of a specific concept or definition? Do you sometimes have the impression of 'holding a half toothless broken comb that you have just dropped'?
+ Does speaking many languages make us more prone to look at interculturality from a more complex way? If you speak several languages, how often do you look at how words related to interculturality as a subject of research and education are connoted/'flavoured'?

In what follows I have collected *bits and pieces* from the fragments; read them through and reflect on what they mean to you:

"All categories essentialise *nolens volens*.".
"Non-essentialism essentialises the human as *superhuman*".

"Interculturality is the enemy of the obvious".

"Any statement on interculturality is ideological. *I am always ideological*".

"Interculturality reminds us that we constantly falsify our claims on the world".

"He believes that the idea of 'European democratic culture' as a substitute for interculturality goes against democratisation of the notion itself".

"The idea is not to create a competitive market of ideas ('the best wins') but to trigger dialogue for change. It is not about substituting an idea with another".

Finally, the chapter fragments contain a certain number of questions that I was asked or asked myself, how would you answer them (you may also refuse to answer them)?

What is interculturality about in the end? What are the expected outcomes of the *inter-* and the *-ality* of the notion?
Why do we feel that we need the concept of 'culture' when we work on interculturality?
What would you like to change about a new article, chapter or book about interculturality that you have just published?

References

Abdallah-Pretceille, M. (2006). Interculturalism as a paradigm for thinking about diversity. *Intercultural Education*, *17*(5), 475–483.
Allport, G. W. (1954). *The nature of prejudice*. Reading, MA: Addison-Wesley.
Althusser, L. (2020). *On ideology*. London: Verso.
Amossy, R. (2002). Introduction to the study of Doxa. *Poetics Today*, *23*(3), 369–394.
Augé, M. (2015). *The future*. London: Verso.
Baker, W. (2022). From intercultural to transcultural communication. *Language and Intercultural Communication*, *22*(3), 280–293. https://doi.org/10.1080/14708477.2021.2001477
Barthes, R. (1972). *Mythologies*. New York: Hill and Wang.
Bergson, H. (1998). *Creative evolution*. New York: Dover Publications. (Original work published 1907)
Borghetti, C., & Qin, X. (2022). Resources for intercultural learning in a non-essentialist perspective: An investigation of student and teacher perceptions in Chinese universities. *Language and Intercultural Communication*, 22(5), 599–614. https://doi.org/10.1080/14708477.2022.2105344
Chemla, K., & Fox Keller, E. (2017). *Cultures without culturalism: The making of scientific knowledge*. Durham, NC and London: Duke University Press.

Cheng, A. (2004). *Can China think?* Paris: Seuil.
Dervin, F. (2016). *Intercultural education: A theoretical and methodological toolbox*. London: Palgrave Macmillan.
Dervin, F. (2021). *Critical and reflexive languaging in the construction of interculturality as an object of research and practice (19 April). Digital series of talks on plurilingualism and interculturality*. Copenhagen: University of Copenhagen.
Dervin, F. (2023). Introduction. In F. Dervin, M. Yuan, & Sude (Eds.), *Teaching interculturality 'otherwise'*. London: Routledge.
Dervin, F., & Jacobsson, A. (2022). *Intercultural communication education. Broken realities and rebellious dreams*. London: Springer.
Dervin, F., & Yuan, M. (2023). *Reflecting on and with the 'more-than-human' in education: Things for interculturality*. Singapore: Springer.
Ferri, G. (2018). *Intercultural communication: Critical approaches, future challenges*. London: Palgrave Macmillan.
Holliday, A. (2011). *Intercultural communication and ideology*. London: SAGE.
Humphreys, G. (2021). Planning, implementing, and evaluating a non-essentialist training programme for study abroad in the Japanese HE context. *Intercultural Communication Education*, 4(2), 155–176.
Itkonen, T., & Dervin, F. (Eds.). (2017). *Silent partners in multicultural education*. Charlotte, NC: IAP.
Kalopissi-Verti, S., & Foskolou, V. (Eds.). (2022). *Intercultural encounters in medieval Greece after 1204: The evidence of art and material culture*. Turnhout: Brepols Publishers.
Minett, A. J., Dietrich, S. E., & Ekici, D. (2022). *Person to person peacebuilding, intercultural communication and English language teaching: Voices from the virtual intercultural borderlands*. Clevedon: Multilingual Matters.
Morin, E. (2021). *Leçons d'un siècle de vie*. Paris: Denoel.
Nietzsche, F. (1989). *Beyond good and evil*. New York: Vintage Books.
Pieterse, J. N. (2020). *Connectivity and global studies*. London: Palgrave Macmillan.
R'boul, H. (2022). Epistemological plurality in intercultural communication knowledge. *Journal of Multicultural Discourses,*, 17, 173–188. https://doi.org/10.1080/17447143.2022.2069784
R'boul, H. (2023). Afterword: Theorizing and teaching interculturality otherwise: What otherwise? In F. Dervin, M. Yuan, & Sude (Eds.), *Teaching interculturality 'otherwise'*. London: Routledge.
Robertson, S. L. (2021). Provincializing the OECD-PISA global competences project. *Globalisation, Societies and Education*, 19(2), 167–182.
Wikan, U. (2001). *Generous betrayal: Politics of culture in new Europe*. Chicago, IL: Chicago University Press.
Wood, P. (2020). *Diversity rules*. New York and London: Encounter Books.
Yildiz, Y. (2013). *Beyond the mother tongue: The postmonolingual condition*. New York: Fordham University Press.
Yuan, M., Dervin, F., Sude, & Chen, N. (2022). *Change and exchange in global education. Learning with Chinese stories of interculturality*. London: Palgrave Macmillan.

3 Stances towards alternative knowledge

'Officially', the complex field of intercultural communication education was created after the Second World War in the 'West' (Kulich et al., 2020) – first in communication studies, diplomacy and business and then education, under different guises. Since the 1980s (and even before that), following critical trends and turns in other fields of research, many 'accepted' ideas have been questioned, discarded and revised – not necessarily for the 'best', though. Culturalism and its companion -isms (essentialism, orientalism) have now become the main targets of many 'Western' researchers and, marginally, within glocal academic and educational contexts outside this sphere (see Abdallah-Pretceille, 1989; Holliday, 2011). So-called 'alternative' knowledge (alternative *from* and *for* whom?) and 'new' turns – which one seems to label happily as 'critical' today – have led to the emergence of different concepts, notions, 'theories', 'paradigms', 'methods' and . . . ideologies which tend to dominate and silence other voices – while claiming to be somewhat 'liberating' (see Xu, 2022). This chapter reviews some stances towards knowledge that is deemed to be 'alternative' today, reminding us of the importance of keeping a critical eye open towards *ALL* assertions, statements and lines of argumentation – even when they are branded as 'critical'.

~ **Fragments II** ~

[Amateur]

> He is a proud amateur of interculturality. An amateur is *someone who likes and gets pleasure from something*. His amateurism is lifelong.

He gets excited by art and music for the thoughts they provide him with for rethinking interculturality.

He wonders where his books would be located in bookstores: which sections and shelves? After checking how his publishers classify his work on

DOI: 10.4324/9781003371052-4
This chapter has been made available under a CC-BY-NC-ND 4.0 license.

their websites, he notes: *education, sociology, philosophy, linguistics, cultural studies* (amongst others). He doesn't think that he fits in any of these but in *all of them*.

[Arrogance]

Saying *I know what interculturality is* and *being certain about what we should do with and about her* 'critically' could be seen as arrogant. Admitting the contrary is questioning (rightly) established power relations.

In dealing with interculturality, we should run away from overconfidence and hysteria, as is often witnessed in many accusations of essentialism. *The essentialist is always the other – never us!* We are all essentialists, although we hate admitting it.

Too many perspectives on interculturality do not aim to 'educate' or 'train' people but to *edify* them – i.e. to instruct them morally . . .

[Change]

We should never push for *interculturality-as-change* – a tautology that reminds us of the transformative characteristic of the notion – if we don't feel that neither of us should do it *together*. Interculturality is always about *you* and *me*.

[Chinese]

Listening to young Chinese students discuss interculturality, he wonders why he would want to continue reading certain strands of research. They energise him with their thought-provoking views and critiques (see an account of such dialogues in Dervin & Tan, 2023).

The more he reads about Chinese discourse instruments from the past, the more he believes that they had figured out interculturality well before 'us' – although the notion did not 'exist' (see e.g. Yuan et al., 2022). *Let's go back to what the past has to say* across *China and the world*.

Someone asks him if he could write a paper about decolonising Chinese language education. He asks them to define *decolonising* and what that could mean for this context – *they don't know*. When he asks them why they have chosen this topic, they reply that *everyone is decolonising* so 'we should also decolonise Chinese'. He tells them that he prefers to remain silent. He has nothing to say. *It is too early to unthink and decolonise decolonising*.

Trying to infuse some 'Chinese right to speak' in intercultural research by retaining UK and US ideologies is a façade that deserves to be renovated. Labelling something as 'Chinese' does not make it 'Chinese'. We need to problematise this idea *together*.

[Cited]

Citing someone who rehearses the same as everybody else in the 'West' because their name sounds like a name from outside the 'centre' is distressing. He would rather they were cited for new (multilingually and critically connoted) knowledge that really makes us feel discomfort *interculturally*. Unfortunately, we still want *comfort* – the same, *our own image!* For him, interculturality is about losing one's own image and trying on different masks.

[Choice]

Once again, someone advises him to change from the label *intercultural* to *transcultural* ("you should start saying *transcultural*," they say). When he asks them why, he hears the same refrain again: "It is more dynamic". But could one be more dynamic than the *inter-* and the *-ality* of interculturality? He believes that a change of label needs to be meaningful. Considering the polysemy of both inter- and transcultural, he does not believe that it is worth it.

On stationery found in English in China he reads: "Don't have to choose! Let it be".

[Curiosity]

Every single person engaging with interculturality should be curious about knowledge from outside the 'West' – not just those from the 'East' or the 'Global South'. Every one of us has an epistemic responsibility to do so.

[Disenfranchise]

We have to listen to other ways of talking about and dealing with social justice. Statements about the importance of social justice in interculturality are far from enough, especially when they disenfranchise us from being *even more* critical. He remembers seeing signs saying 'this place believes in social justice' popping up at a Finnish university one day. Wanting to test the 'strength' of this assertion, he stopped a 'university leader' in front of one of these signs and claimed that he had been the victim of discrimination. The 'leader' was speechless. He kept looking at the sign on purpose. When he asked him what to do, the 'leader' replied that he wasn't too sure and would get back to him about it – he never did.

[Divide]

Interculturality does not draw any conclusion of its own.

The universality of technological use is a complete illusion. The world is in fact divided between different types of applications, websites and social media, which some people will never use. *This intercultural divide cannot be ignored.* Many a times during the pandemic he was told that he could not use a given app because it was banned by one institution and/ or a country. Technology seems to reflect well the state of interculturality today: *Divided, segregated* and *unfair*. We live in different worlds, with some fragile overlaps.

While Europe is 'spreading' her own ideology of *democratic culture* as a substitute for interculturality (negating the *inter-* and *-ality* and replacing culture with another ideologeme – a piece of ideology, see Council of Europe, 2016) the Chinese have started problematising intercultural education as 传播效果 (chuánbò xiàoguǒ) which translates as *dissemination, spreading effect, propagation effect* (see 外语教育中的跨文化能力教学参考框架 – *A Framework of Reference for Intercultural Competence in Foreign Language Education*, SISU, 2022). Training people for interculturality becomes a way of teaching them *how to disseminate knowledge* about China, Chinese culture and Chinese people – i.e. to correct misconceptions. Yes, we should identify untruths to revise the doxa. *But what to do with them?* Replace them with other untruths – because we can never really describe the complexities of each and every one of us? The *inter-* and the *-ality* disappear here, too. In both contexts, intercultural education could become a technology of propaganda and could lead to further divisions *interculturally*. For Gide (1954, p. 1233): "Believe those who are seeking the truth. Doubt those who find it" (translation of "Croyez ceux qui cherchent la vérité, doutez de ceux qui la trouvent").

[Emancipate]

We need new concepts for interculturality. We are still using the same old ones. Let's be creative.

Reading a postcolonial scholar from the South, I still 'feel' 'Western' flavours in the way they present and express their critiques in English. It is as if they were wearing a Western mask uttering critiques 'beyond the West' (see Fanon's (2021) *Black Skin, White Masks*). *How to emancipate? Can we emancipate?*

We have the right to speak, listen to and negotiate, but do we have the power to be listened to and to be taken seriously?

The pseudo-rationalism that tends to govern interculturality in research and education contributes to destroy interculturality itself. The notion should be treated with *poetry* and *active dreaming*.

The (temporary) joy in hearing a Chinese student say: "What I understood through your work is that interculturality is not Western but that we can all contribute knowledge on interculturality".

[Global South]

Who is part of the Global South (and the Global North for that matter)? Who decides? Who has the right to refuse to be categorised under these labels? A Chinese colleague of mine was very surprised when she was asked to take part in a panel discussion about 'epistemic injustice' between the Global South and Global North. She wondered where she stood as a Chinese scholar since she had never heard of these 'Western' fabricated labels. *Ideological clashes and mis-drawering.*

The litany of *the episteme from the South* is a bit disappointing when it still rehearses dominating ideological drills cooked up in the West.

A 'critical' scholar from the Global South uses the voice of a 'critical' scholar from the North to justify the argument that Global Southerners need to claim English in their own conditions, needs and terms. Even here the North tells 'them' what to do!

A friend from the Global South tells him that two 'big names' of interculturality from the UK had mentioned their work in their latest book. After congratulating them, he asked: *What do they do with your work? Where are you located in their work? How 'central' are your ideas? Do they take the critical points they 'borrow' from you seriously throughout their book/ article? How, in all reality, do you disrupt their work? Or are they using you as a mere 'token'?*

Victory should always be tempered with.

[Ignorance as an excuse]

"I can't speak at your event because I don't know anything about Chinese Minzu education". *But you know about diversity and interculturality as a specialist of intercultural education? Minzu education is all about this; you will just have to renegotiate meanings, connotations and ideologies; to listen to others; to ask questions – to 'do' interculturality!* Ignorance as an excuse for not engaging with the other's knowledge – *or for another (political-economic) reason?*

[International]

Calling research 'international' does not make it really *international*. Who speaks? Who is allowed to speak? Who *really* takes part in 'international research'?

[Knowledge]

We must act against knowledge asymmetry in intercultural research and education. Do we have the right to decide how others should/could do interculturality as researchers (a question to himself)?

We must accept that we don't know and that *we can't know*. No one really knows *but* everybody knows. Knowing interculturality vs. (un)knowing *about* interculturality.

When we separate art, music, philosophy and research into different categories, we divide knowledge and the pleasure of learning. Let's reassemble them to save ourselves from insanity.

As scholars, we have a duty to carefully evaluate the kind of knowledge that we produce, use and disseminate. *Criticality of criticality* (Dervin, 2022).

[Liberation]

Disrupt!

We should never force people to speak about interculturality the way we want ourselves to engage with the notion. Intercultural research is full of 'shackles' that we need to shake off. We should never be a prisoner of the way we see interculturality. He has heard too many students recite and rehearse what they think their professors want them to say about interculturality. *Liberate them!*

In a similar vein, we must liberate our readers from the orders dominating their thoughts about interculturality – and from the ones we are imposing on them!

[Noise]

Irony: Those who are entitled to speak about interculturality are noisy about it. Those who experience it remain quiet. Their voices are often manipulated and moulded by the loud speakers.

The noise around interculturality in research and education tends to be monotonous as it rehearses the same litanies. We need heteroclite music instead . . .

[Periphery]

The music of Pierre Boulez (1925–2016) as interculturality. His piece entitled *Rituel* (1974–1975/1987) contains clear influences from Japanese Gogaku and *Sur Incises* (1994) Balinese music, which he *mélanged* with his work. Where are these diverse voices in the intercultural ritornellos of research? Ritornellos of interculturality sound special in *different* rooms with *different* acoustics.

A colleague writes to him apologising for not having included more recent work from him in an article that she was submitting. She mentions two of his references from the early 2010s. He replies that it does not matter. He is not interested in people pushing through his work. However, he had one request: *To include literature beyond the 'centre' and from more recent years.*

Down with pretending to be generous with other voices and letting them talk about interculturality! In the end, *who is really listening?*

The centre still decides what ideology is acceptable/a must for interculturality. The overuse and abuse of terms such as *non-essentialism, citizenship, democracy* in current 'Western' scholarship of interculturality, spreading to the rest of the world, make it obvious (see Porto, 2014). To be part of this limited discursive world, you must recite and use these terms. *If not, you cannot get in; you are rejected.*

If you are from the 'Global South', they welcome you. They want to show how generous they are. However, if you disagree with them and voice too many critiques that can damage their names and reputations, the gates will close . . .

How to disrupt hegemonies for real? Is this a fantasy or a real wish?

[Phobia]

Interculturalspeak-phobia: a (disagreeable) neologism to describe the dislike and fear of certain (automatic) ways of engaging with interculturality in research and education. We all use some form of interculturalspeak (Dervin, 2016) – but the other's 'speak' is often looked down upon.

So-called 'critical' approaches also create stereotypes (e.g. non-essentialism).

[Terrae Incognitae]

As a consequence of specific Western ideologies about interculturality being imposed and preferred in the world of research, some *terrae incognitae* (unknown territories) of interculturality are cut off from view. *Ideological occultation?* As such Chinese Minzu 'ethnic' ideologies are *terrae incognitae* for the West – the unknown. He has argued that they can help us rethink interculturality for ourselves (Dervin & Yuan, 2021).

~ Interthinking ~

Let us start this interthinking session by reviewing the keywords that I used in introducing the fragments. Here is a full list: *Amateur, Arrogance, Change, Chinese, Cited, Choice, Curiosity, Disenfranchise, Divide, Emancipate, Global South, Ignorance as an excuse, International, Knowledge, Liberation, Noise, Periphery, Phobia*, Terrae incognitae. For each keyword, try to remember what arguments and critiques were shared in the fragments and what they mean. The keywords contain three verbs of action – *Disenfranchise, Divide, Emancipate* – what do they tell us about stances about alternative knowledge?

Now spend some time exploring these questions, and provide as many answers as you can:

+ How much of the 'alternative' knowledge of interculturality discussed in this chapter are you familiar with? Try to remember how you came across such knowledges.
+ Are you aware of any current ideological divides in the way interculturality is 'done' in research and education globally? How familiar are you with some of the *terrae incognitae* of interculturality from different parts of the world (see Menon, 2022)?
+ How often do you link up the way you research, study, teach about interculturality to history? What perspectives has this 'archaeological' work brought to you?
+ The argument that interculturality is always about *you* and *me* is somewhat obvious. However, this 'hyphen' is not always taken into consideration in research and education, often 'bending' towards one pole of this continuum. Do you try to include *you-me* systematically in the way you problematise, interpret and analyse interculturality?

+ How eager are you to experience discomfort in the ways you engage with interculturality in research and education? Have such moments allowed you to move forward in your thinking about the notion?
+ Is art or music (or any other 'activity' not labelled as 'research') a source of inspiration for unthinking and rethinking interculturality for you? Try to recall specific moments when, for example, a work of art made you think 'otherwise' about the notion.
+ How to 'liberate' ourselves from our (limited) knowledge of interculturality as a subject of research and education, even when we think we are 'doing' her critically?

Review the following short excerpts from the fragments reflecting on your own practices as a researcher, a student, a teacher, a social being:

> "We are all essentialists although we hate admitting it".
> "The (temporary) joy in hearing a Chinese student tell me: 'What I understood through your work is that interculturality is not Western, but that we can all contribute knowledge on interculturality'".
> "Knowing interculturality vs. (un)knowing *about* interculturality".
> "The noise around interculturality in research and education tends to be monotonous as it rehearses the same litanies".
> "Ritornellos of interculturality sound special in *different* rooms with *different* acoustics".

A certain number of neologisms and 'new' terms were proposed in the chapter. I have selected five that I would like you to review. How do you understand them? Have you come across concepts that are reminiscent of them? How much could they help you unthink and rethink your engagement with the very notion of interculturality?

> Criticality of criticality
> Ideological clashes
> Ideological occultation
> Interculturality-as-change
> Interculturalspeak-phobia.

References

Abdallah-Pretceille, M. (1989). *L'éducation interculturelle*. Paris: QSJ PUF.
Council of Europe. (2016). *Reference framework of competences for democratic culture (RFCDC)*. www.coe.int/en/web/reference-framework-of-competences-for-democratic-culture/home

Dervin, F. (2016). *Intercultural education: A theoretical and methodological toolbox*. London: Palgrave Macmillan.
Dervin, F. (2022). *Interculturality in fragments: A reflexive approach*. Singapore: Springer.
Dervin, F., & Tan, H. (2023). *Supercriticality and interculturality*. Singapore: Springer.
Dervin, F., & Yuan, M. (2021). *Revitalizing interculturality: Minzu as a companion*. London: Routledge.
Fanon, F. (2021). *Black skin, White masks*. London: Penguin Classics.
Gide, A. (1954). *Journal volume 2.1926–1950*. Paris: Gallimard.
Holliday, A. (2011). *Intercultural communication and ideology*. London: SAGE.
Kulich, S. J., Weng, L., Tong, R., & DuBois, G. (2020). Interdisciplinary history of intercultural communication studies. In D. Landis & D. P. S. Bhawuk (Eds.), *The Cambridge handbook of intercultural training* (pp. 60–163). Cambridge: Cambridge University Press.
Menon, D. M. (2022). *Changing theory: Concepts from the global south*. New Delhi: Routledge India.
Porto, M. (2014). Intercultural citizenship education in an EFL online project in Argentina. *Language and Intercultural Communication, 14*, 245–261.
SISU (2022). *A framework of reference for intercultural competence in Foreign Language Education*. (2022). Shanghai: Shanghai Foreign Language Education Press.
Xu, X. (2022). Epistemic diversity and cross-cultural comparative research: Ontology, challenges, and outcomes. *Globalisation, Societies and Education, 20*(1), 36–48. https://doi.org/10.1080/14767724.2021.1932438
Yuan, M., Dervin, F., Sude, & Chen, N. (2022). *Change and exchange in global education. Learning with Chinese stories of interculturality*. London: Palgrave Macmillan.

4 The Achilles' heels of interculturality

Flawed invulnerability is a theme found in many stories from around the world – from the Ossetian warrior Sosruko to Celtic hero Diarmuid. Achilles, whose story is found in Homer's *The Iliad* (1987), was a heroic warrior in Ancient Greece, whose famous story has to do with being invisible. Different narratives around his famous 'heel' are found in the literature. The most famous one has to do with how a nymph wanted to immortalise her son (Achilles) by holding him by his left ankle while dipping him in a river of eternal life. That spot, his heel, became his weak spot since it wasn't dipped into the water. Achilles dies in a battle when his heel is pierced by Paris' arrow. Achilles' heel thus refers to weaknesses in what might appear as 'strong' and 'powerful'. The multiple fields attached to the notion of interculturality have 'existed' ranging from 40 to 80 years in the 'West' (for a history of the study of language and intercultural communication, see Jackson, 2014). Some have built up strong profiles (e.g. language and intercultural communication) while others are still emerging (e.g. intercultural philosophy – maybe). After decades of what is often described as 'simplistic', 'culturalist' and promoting 'methodological nationalism' in most of these fields, more 'critical' perspectives have emerged, as we have already discussed (see Xie, 2014; Atay et al., 2020). In the previous chapters we have explored some 'doxic' elements as well as stances towards alternative knowledges today. This chapter helps us deepen our critiques and understanding of where we stand with interculturality in research and education today by exploring some Achilles' heels of the notion.

~ **Fragments III** ~

[Administration]

Move away from administrative-like perspectives on interculturality: *Jargon, orders, control* and *empty slogans*. Even worse are administrative-like utterances disguised under discourses of research.

All the competition created by academia to publish, obtain funds – *admin-like* – could kill creativity. Slow pace is needed to engage with interculturality seriously.

[Anchor]

There seems to be a tendency to be geo-politically anchored and thus divided in the voices that we include and use to deal with interculturality in research. After listening to 15 scholars from different parts of the 'West' in 2021, he could see clearly this trend in the references that they mentioned in their lectures. These 'anchors' – which overlap a little at times amongst scholars – also show that the 'West' is divided ideologically about interculturality in research and education.

At times, 'our' vision of interculturality pulls us down like an anchor.

[Bouvard and Pécuchet]

The Bouvard and Pécuchet syndrome of interculturality: *Reviews of reviews of reviews of... previous research*. No new research, no creativity, *just reviews*. Reviews are not a problem as such, but they need (at least) to go beyond one's own or nearby fields to be useful.

Are we doomed to be like Bouvard and Pécuchet, the two characters from Flaubert's (1976) novel, who try to explore the world of ideas and learn everything they can about all kinds of fields of knowledge, but fail disgracefully at the end?

Isn't there a future for interculturality if we try? Knowledge about interculturality is overwhelming in research but also in fiction, the arts, everyday life experience. *Let's explore and disregard the fear of failing!*

[Cage]

This powerful quote from Kafka (1954, p. 54): "A cage went in search of a bird". Replace *bird* with *interculturality*.

He reads a chapter written by someone from applied linguistics about interculturality. References are only made to (Western) applied linguists to justify arguments made by the author about interculturality. These references rehearse, often clumsily, what scholars in other fields claimed decades before and from which they have already moved away. Field-centrism and a lack of archaeological knowledge beyond one's own corner of the world are in fact *enemies* to interculturality. Interculturality urges us to be constantly inquisitive.

Why are we made to believe that thinking in 'wholes' is the only valid way to do scholarship on interculturality? The artificiality of this obsession is already slaughtering research, especially the creativity that should go with it. *The imposing structure before floating ideas. The cage before an open intellectual landscape.*

Language is also like a prison when we speak of interculturality. *Say the word and you are caged.* Language can censor our curiosity in research.

"You should make a model for interculturality, Fred" – For him this means: "you should cage interculturality". The notion is already too 'hijacked' and 'kidnapped' to add a 'model' to her. The word *model* is based on a Latin word that derives itself from the Proto-Indo-European root *med-* for 'take appropriate measures'. *Who can decide what is appropriate for interculturality globally when the notion is so polysemous and economic-politically multifaceted?* Proposing a model could attract more citations and fame (see Peng et al., 2020). *He prefers hiding in the shade.*

Research on interculturality is now a mixed bag of doxa, 'science' and militancy (fervour, advocacy). While we are busy discoursing and reducing her, interculturality plays hide and seek with us – but we still pretend to be her 'master'.

[Capitalism]

Interculturality is central in the making of capitalism. We all believe and yet pretend that she is about *peace, amity, social justice* but she is also for profit – *ours, theirs, yours*. In the end, someone will always gain and/or earn (and lose!) something.

[Certainties]

Tone down our certainties and certitudes. For Barthes (1985), there are three types of arrogance: *Doxa, science, militancy*. All three seem to be fully covered by research and education on interculturality.

[Change]

Why are we uncomfortable with the idea that *everything changes constantly*? Is it because it makes us feel helpless, incapable of controlling what is happening to us, to others, to the world, to . . . interculturality? Looking at the state of the world today, we are not in control *in any case*. *Kinetophobia* is, according to Papastergiadis (2012), the fear of movement. People researching and educating for interculturality must be trained for *kinetophilia* – to love moving away from their own ideas and those dominating our thoughts globally.

[Children]

Why is it that many of us believe that we cannot learn anything about interculturality *from* children? Looking at the world in summer 2022, he is not convinced that 'we' adults know what we are doing about it (war, racism, polarisation, hypercentrisms . . .) (see Jacobsson et al., 2023).

[Chinese]

Jin Yong's (2018) book *Legends of the Condor Heroes*' back cover says: "A Chinese *Lord of the Rings*". In order to sell, one must compare to and gauge with the Global 'West'. In research, it is time to promote *Lord of the Rings* as follows: "A 'Western' *Legends of the Condor Heroes*". Think 'otherwise'.

[Circulation]

The one-sided circulation of ideas needs disrupting. He is giving a keynote this week. All the other speakers look like him: *White, top universities* and *implanted into the Western English-scape*. He never looks at himself in the mirror; he prefers to see others when it comes to interculturality.

Stop kidnapping and hijacking ideas and terms! Stop 'reinventing' not just wheels but, especially, already *broken ones*!

[Cited]

Why do we write about interculturality in the end? He guesses: *To dominate, to try to get our voice out there, to make space for ourselves, to experience (maybe) some (temporary) fame, to hear "oh you're that Dervin!", to be quoted, worshipped, to be swallowed by the other, to make them become us?* But being cited is never a sign of victory. Only if those who quote us engage with our ideas, question them, disagree with them, wish to discard them, can we celebrate (temporarily)!

[Citizen of the world]

(Seen in a scholar's biodata) "he is a native of XX (city in Europe) and a citizen of the world".

Self-aggrandising! Can we ever be a 'citizen' of the world? What does this 'sloganesque' word really mean? *De-mystify the idea of the citizen of the world.*

[Clutches]

We want to find out about and 'possess' interculturality because we are afraid of the void and the unknown.

Research on interculturality is full of centrisms: *Western-centrism, adult-centrism, guru-centrism, concept-centrism, ideology-centrism, institution-centrism, field-centrism* . . . They all blind us in front of the inexhaustible diversities of the notion.

Get rid of intellectual 'clutches'!

Many scholars of interculturality behave like pantomimes – a word from Latin (*pantomimus*) which means *imitators of everything*. One day one is an essentialist, the other a fervent non-essentialist. One day one is *transcultural*, the other *decolonial*. One day one tries to 'conquer' the European market with one intercultural ideology sponsored by the EU, another the same economic-political entity provides one with money to try to 'reach out' to the Chinese market, using the symbolic power of European universities to 'entice' Chinese scholars (if China invested money to spread a specific ideology of interculturality in Europe, they would be stopped at the door of Europe straightaway. *Ideological injustice*).

Spectralon is a diffuse reflectance material – making it maybe the whitest material in the world. When hit by light, it reflects 99% of it. A suitable new label for current research on interculturality – even for many of those of us labelling what we do as *decolonial*. Instead of 'spectraloning' our way into research, we could make use of antireflective coating to reduce 'white' reflection.

[Consume]

In musical phrases, an *ostinato* refers to recurring frequently, *repeated*. So many ostinatos in intercultural research: One repeats again and again the same words, same ideologies and same names. We do consume a lot of knowledge about interculturality today, but how much do we produce? The question of production should be first – not just mere consumption, copy and repetition.

Down with procrustean thinking and conformity in research on interculturality, which disregards individuality and specificities. The Greek legend of Procrustes tells us how the robber compelled his victims to lie on his iron bed, and cut off their legs, hammered, racked their bodies to fit the size of the bed, leading to their death – *time to get rid of this evil!*

[Definition]

Trying to define interculturality is barking up the wrong tree. Definitions make us feel comfortable and give us the illusion that we can 'grab' and 'possess'. *Destroy definitions*. To define is in a sense to prevent oneself from thinking further, *to close up shop*.

Approach a subject without a definition and observe what it is instead. Is there really a need to (re-)define interculturality when the notion itself begs us to not do that?

[Door]

The Real McCoy: When you work on interculturality in research, you don't close the door at the end of the day and say "It's over! Done for today".

Advice from a senior scholar: "Find a community of people who share your own values for your research". In other words: Retract yourself into a community where you can bask under the same ideological sun and never engage with alternatives, never change your views, never disrupt your take on interculturality. Close the doors and feel safe. *The end*.

'Theories of interculturality' constitute a mere *Weltanschauung*, a (falsely) comprehensive conception or apprehension of the world from a particular standpoint. *A closed worldview*.

Reading and writing about interculturality is oppressive – so many ideologies of which we might not be aware but use in our work; they hit us in the face but we don't feel the pain instantly. Delayed pain. *Let's protect ourselves!*

[Face-to-face]

Someone from Brazil invites him to give a keynote. He suggests doing it online since traveling to Brazil for a couple of days would be too exhausting and not especially environmentally friendly. They reply that it would be "too expensive for them to organise an online talk" for him and that they would prefer that he visits them. *He refuses*. Have we not learnt anything from the pandemic? Do we still believe that *only* face-to-face is the right way to 'do' interculturality? He has met thousands of people at conferences and seminars and often felt that he was wasting his time – as much as most of these people probably felt the same. He does not feel the need to meet people 'face-to-face' anymore. Our faces are still there, *even online*. He notes that in Chinese face-to-face translates as 面对面 (miànduìmiàn). 面 means face, surface, but also to meet and personally. The character shows the outline of the face with eyes in the middle part. Interestingly, the same character also refers to flour and noodles (the original character for noodles was simplified and 'merged' with face in the 20th century). He sees noodles as a good metaphor for the complexities and 'messy' impression of seeing the other 'face-to-face' and/or online. When we are together online, we are also enmeshed in the 'noodles' of co-constructing who we are.

[Fly]

He believes that looking at Chinese Minzu 'ethnic' education (Sude et al., 2020) through Americanised perspectives makes no sense (e.g. 'multicultural education', 'culturally-responsive education'). These perspectives fly past each other, gazing at their mere appearances. Sometimes the globally dominating perspective lands and 'lectures' the other on how they should understand who they are and what they should do. This often leads to (transformed, idealised) ideological mimetism but also . . . clashes.

[Geopolitics of interculturality]

When we talk about interculturality in research, we should specify: *US* intercultural communication education, *European Union* intercultural education. Or even *Byramian, Gorskian, Hollidayian, Hofstedian, Dervinian* . . . intercultural (communication) (education). *ELFian, language educationian, teacher educationian*, could be added. Ideally, new labels such as *Atayian, Chenian, R'boulian* as well as *Atayorskian, Chollidayian, R'Dervinian* could also be in use in the field.

[Good]

Can we be good at interculturality?
He repeats: *NO*. Since we do not understand the notion the same way, influenced by our ideologically tainted glasses from various economic-political spheres, we would never be able to agree on what being *good at* might mean. And even if we agree, there is no guarantee that it would work. Human beings are too unstable and prone to performing to make it happen.

[Gurus]

The more idolised, the more ideologised.

Do we really need to think (only) through big names and gurus for dealing with interculturality?

Someone tells him that he is himself a *guru* in research on interculturality. *Is he?* A guru has followers – *He doesn't* and *he does not want any*. He always makes sure that his own students don't see him or treat him as one (to the disappointment of some of them). A guru is supported by strong (half-hidden) forces such as governments or supranational organisations – *He is not*. He 'just' has his University of Helsinki identity. He rejects any offer of cooperating with big organisations. A guru is somewhat consistent as far as the 'orders' they give to their followers – *he frequently 'transforms' his views on interculturality, which makes following him challenging.*

We must rebel against our gurus and our ideas!

Run away from gurus, tribes and courts! They can prevent *the inter-* from happening!

[Ideas]

After reading a so-called 'decolonial' paper on interculturality: *A good ideologically representative soup made of sweet 'white' ingredients pretending to be durian ice cream* (cultivated in some parts of Asia, durian has a sweet flavour but pungent odour).

Interesting: He has noticed that many ads for online talks present us with *a title* for the talks and *long biodatas*, but he rarely sees any abstract. *Name, production* and *capitals* before *ideas*?

At times, interculturality is a repository of frozen ideas.

What is *an idea* in intercultural research?

[Imagination]

An example of ideo-maginary (ideological imaginary): *Individuals who are highly interculturally competent have more ethnorelativistic cultural worldviews and cosmopolitan outlooks.* Every other word derives from a 'Western' ideological position in this assertion: *Interculturally competent, ethnorelativistic cultural worldviews* and *cosmopolitan outlooks*. As we read through these words, names of scholars, geopolitical locations and political takes spring in front of our eyes.

Methodological interculturalism: Placing our own ideological take on interculturality at the centre, brushing aside other ideologies – and labelling them as 'ideological' while referring to ours as 'theoretical', 'conceptual'.

"Essentialism is bad, and so is liberal multicultural education". Are there such clear-cut positions? Who are the real people behind these imagined figures?

Theatres of the imagination.

The overuse of the verb to *reimagine* in research today: Can we reimagine when we rehearse the same as others? Imagining means to leave things as 'they are' behind and to rearrange, reshape and rebuild them, randomly and aimlessly. *How often do we do this for interculturality?* Have you ever had a dream that was coherent and understandable?

[Job]

Interculturality is neither a profession nor a quality.

[Jump]

There appears to be a lot of opportunism in the way people 'jump at' intercultural topics in research and education. *Profit at the end . . .*

Interculturality is disjunct; it jumps all over the place; it is uncontrollable. He reads some research on interculturality. He feels nothing. *Cold. Morbidity, at times.* He experiences interculturality. *He is alive. He feels, he loves, he is jubilant!*

[Making demands]

A scholar to another: "I agree with the demands you are making on educators".

1 The demands are not the scholar's since they just repeat what the one speaking here has said before (*his* demands disguised as *his interlocutor's*).
2 Should scholars make 'demands' on educators when it comes to interculturality? Could this disenfranchise scholars from following demands made on them by others?

[Mistakes]

We all make mistakes! *Scholars included.* Accept it, talk about it, be honest. *Atelophilia*, or the appreciation of making mistakes: A good principle for researchers and educators specialising in interculturality.

[Nausea]

Reading a couple of recent chapters on interculturality in education, he feels nauseous. *Words, concepts, ideas, are repeated robot-like.* What is hiding behind all this in the end?

[Orders]

A world that is Western- and adult-centric governing the way we think and do interculturality is extremely suspicious. Stand off from the position of the one who knows and, especially, the one who gives orders.

The current 'technologies' created by research for interculturality (e.g. the sempiternal idea of intercultural competence) tend to remove humanity from the human. No tolerance for improvisation, flexibility or incoherence. All programmed. *All orders to follow.*

He keeps giving orders to his readers. *Orders to not give orders constitute ORDERS.* One cannot talk about interculturality without giving (our) orders!

When he says that interculturality should be 'reciprocal', is he assuming that this is the 'right' thing to do, *his order*?

We are mere passive spectators to the dominance of interculturality.

[Path]

First, we need to block off our normal path of thinking.

[Pigeonholing]

Is there a difference between intercultural communication and interculturality? The only difference is that they are pigeonholed and tagged differently.

Pigeonholing interculturality into 'neat' scientific categories to make sure that she fits somewhere is awkward.

He notices that a colleague whom he had labelled as *a linguist* is also a professor of intercultural education – but they have never published anything on the intercultural. Is he also an impostor as *a professor of 'multicultural' education*? Is he the epitome of the double-bind?

[Placebo]

Non-essentialism is like Balzac's (1831/2012) *Peau de Chagrin* ('The Skin of Sorrow'/'The Wild Ass's Skin'), in which a young man acquires a 'magical' piece of Chagrin in a shop. The skin will fulfil any wish, shrinking each time a wish is granted, until it disappears with its owner dying. Like the Peau de Chagrin, non-essentialism can be treacherous if we are too greedy . . .

Could research on interculturality be a placebo for something else?

[Playground]

Intercultural scholarship is still a playground for the privileged – even when we pretend to be critical and hijack (in the process) e.g. decoloniality in our 'own' terms (see a convincing counter-example in Montejo's (2021) *Maya-logue*, in which he urges us to consider an Indigenous Maya perspective).

[Power]

To fight against selected abuses of power is a noble endeavour. But to fight against *all powers* – our own included – is even better. Vilification of essentialism is a distraction from those still eager to keep their power to speak for and over others. *Don't essentialise!* They lecture them. We have the power to tell others.

By looking down upon and negating other ways of thinking about the notion, Eurocentric discourses of interculturality are often close to neo-racism, considering that other ways of engaging with her are 'inferior' and not worthy of consideration. *'Our' democracy and citizenship must not be disturbed.*

[(The) power of disagreements]

Does it matter if we don't see and perceive things the same way? *No, it does not.* We must accept the power of disagreements.

Non-essentialism is morbid. It kills any possibility to disagree, the excitement to enter into a friendly and healthy argument.

[Preachiness]

Preachiness (to advocate, urge acceptance/compliance with) is what we tend to do in intercultural research and education. There could be an echo of what is happening in the field of interculturality today in this

Greek myth where a woman was deprived of speaking, and all she could do was repeat what others had said.

He read a paper that says: *This course will shape their values, beliefs and identity as a global citizen.* Straightaway he is thinking, *Propaganda.*

Considering the fact that we constantly adapt to what we say to others, and at times lie, manipulate and use others for our own (monetary) benefits, how could we trust any take on interculturality? What is the real motivation for someone to assert anything about the notion in research and education? Some of us make money out of *our words* (our preaching), selling books, articles, getting salary increases, promotions, being invited to talks, being flown around the world, etc.

They start calling for *polycentric* and *decolonial* voices to be heard while continuing their privileged monologues.

Enhancing, decolonising, reimagining, transforming, reconceptualising . . . interculturality beyond [re-]claims wanted.

He saw the word *havism* printed on someone's T-shirt today. A great -*ism* for intercultural research and education for describing the dominating ideologies of owning, possessing, grabbing, being entitled to, holding – in short: making interculturality ours, and *ours only.*

[Publishing]

What is the main motivation for publishing articles today? Following a few e-communities of scholars online, he would say: 1. *To show off*, 2. *To get promoted (and get more money, prestige and power)*, 3. *To be admired*, 4. *To make others jealous*. Contributing to (new) knowledge rarely appears to be the (promoted) motivation. Spelling out what the real 'new' contribution is appears to be even rarer.

Can we say anything 'new' about interculturality?
He asked some colleagues working on interculturality who they write for, who *that* reader they have in mind is when they write – *nobody*, they replied. *They just write.* Our readers as ghosts haunting our work, roaming our pages, being invisible. *Include readers.*

[Rupture]

Non-essentialism (often confused with anti-essentialism) will lead to the inertia of the field of interculturality or even its destruction. Where else can we go when we look into what the human is not about? He is not sure if we can consider that there have been real 'ruptures', real 'changes' in research on interculturality over the last decades. *Imitation, repetition, devotion, self-promotion, illusions.*

[Speak]

A lot is spoken about interculturality (and its companions) today. But do we really speak or just *utter* words? What is it that we are really talking about? Are we really talking? *The power to speak but also the power to listen to* and *to be listened to!*

The word *discourse* comes from Latin *discursus* for a running about, from the past participle of *discurrere*, to run about, run to and fro, hasten. In Proto-Indo-European, the root *kers-* meant *to run*. Any discourse on interculturality is running to and fro, in all directions, and should be taken as such. Any discourse on interculturality is incoherent, related to ideologies from *here and there*.

[Tokens]

Tokens (the other from the East or the Global South used to confirm dominating 'Western' ideologies – not to disrupt them) can contribute to recolonising and strengthening the grip of the powerful. *Detokenising* interculturality is central in *decolonising* her.

[Truth]

One research paper claims to examine how students "establish successful cooperation" interculturally. He wonders: From whose perspective can *success* be assessed? What if students perform their cooperation as *successful* for their teacher? Do we all see success the same way? What does *success* mean? Isn't *failure* a good thing, too? *Is research about evaluating success in interculturality thus pushing only one side of the coin?*

To hold the truth in French is *détenir la vérité*. *Détenir* is also found in the idea of keeping someone in jail or sending them to jail (*en détension*). Speaking about interculturality does not necessarily mean speaking the truth. Like all discourses, interculturality is (re-)negotiated, (un-)spoken between us. Thus one 'slice' of discourse might be contradicted by another within seconds.

[Violence]

All these discourses of *citizenship* and *democracy* in intercultural communication education feel so violent at the moment (e.g. Martin et al., 2021). They exclude *de jure* many scholars and educators from corners of the world other than the European village.

[Way of life]

Working on interculturality in research and education is not a job but a way of life.

[Xu Bing]

Chinese artist Xu Bing's reinvented Chinese characters are (rightly) destabilising. We think that they are Chinese, but they are not. The artist designed a calligraphic system based on the English language but resembling Chinese characters, which he calls *Square Word Calligraphy*. One can read the characters by decomposing each letter from the English alphabet. This occurs with confusion, dilly-dallying and even apprehension. Interculturality must function the same way in research and education.

~ Interthinking ~

To start this interthinking section, go back to the fragments and/or your notes and make a list of the Achilles' heels of interculturality that you have identified. Once the list is ready, try to 'rank' them in terms of gravity, awkwardness, capacity to be solved.

Now take some time to reflect on the following questions:

+ Choose your favourite scholar of intercultural communication education and review for yourself the change they have presented in how they problematise and conceptualise interculturality. Focus for example on the concepts that they have used, the ideologies that they have supported and promoted ('orders') and the references that they make to other scholars. What do you notice? How many of the potential transformations that you note have influenced your own work?
+ Have you ever experienced situations of 'symbolic violence' while reading a research paper or a book on interculturality? In other words: have you ever felt stereotyped, excluded and/or discriminated against?

+ Let's come back to the issue of 'money'. In one fragment I wrote: "We all pretend that it is about e.g. peace, amity, social justice but, in the end, it is for profit – *ours, theirs, yours*". What do you make of this argument?
+ What does otherwise between inverted commas mean to you in *thinking interculturality 'otherwise'*?
+ Do you feel that you can clearly separate your role and experiences as a scholar, teacher, student of interculturality and as a person 'doing' interculturality on a daily basis? I used the metaphor of the 'door' in one fragment – can you easily close the door between these positions?

These are selected short excerpts from the fragments. Review them one by one and try to explain your own position in relation to the excerpts – and why not: how you could take them into account in your engagement with interculturality:

> "Trying to define interculturality is barking at the wrong tree".
> "Language is also like a prison when we speak of interculturality".
> "At times, interculturality is a repository of frozen ideas".
> "Slow pace is needed to engage with interculturality seriously".
> "We are mere passive spectators to the dominance of interculturality".
> "The 'West' is divided ideologically about interculturality in research and education".

I would also like to ask you the following questions from the fragments. If I answered them in the fragments, compare your answers to mine:

What is *an idea* in intercultural research?
Does it matter if we don't see, perceive things the same way?
What is the real motivation for someone to assert anything about the notion in research and education?
Can we say anything 'new' about interculturality?
Isn't *failure* a good thing in interculturality too?

To finish this chapter and as a transition to Part II, where we shall explore some ways of tackling some of the issues noted in Chapters 2, 3 and 4, I suggest that you choose a paper published recently in *Language and Intercultural Communication; Intercultural Education; Journal of Intercultural Studies; International Journal of Intercultural Relations; Journal of Multicultural Discourses*. Read it carefully, paying attention to the 'voices' that the authors introduce and manipulate in the paper. Check the list of references and try to make sense of who the scholars are (*Where from? Gender? Institutional affiliation? Languages used in their work? Multilingual publications?*). If you identify a scholar from the Global South in the list of references (a scholar working *IN* the Global South or *FROM* the Global South but based *IN* the Global North), check how the paper's author 'uses' their voice. *What do they make them say and do and for what purpose(s)?*

References

Atay, A., & Chen, Y.-W. (Eds.). (2020). *Postcolonial turn and geopolitical uncertainty: Transnational critical intercultural communication pedagogy*. New York: Lexington Books.
Balzac, H. de (2012). *The wild ass's skin*. Oxford: OUP. (Original work published 1831)
Barthes, R. (1985). *The grain of the voice. Interviews 1965–1980*. New York: Hill & Wang.
Flaubert, G. (1976). *Bouvard and Pécuchet*. London: Penguin Classics.
Homer (1987). *The Iliad*. London: Penguin Classics.
Jackson, J. (2014). *Introducing language and intercultural communication*. London: Routledge.
Jacobsson, A., Layne, H., & Dervin, F. (2023). *Children and interculturality in education*. London: Routledge.
Kafka, F. (1954). *Dearest father. Stories and other writings*. New York: Schocken Books.
Martin, T. J., Esteve-Faubel, J. M., & Esteve-Faubel, R. P. (2021). Developing intercultural citizenship competences in higher education by using a literary excerpt in an English as a Foreign Language (EFL) context. *Intercultural Education, 32*(6), 649–666.
Montejo, V. (2021). *Mayalogue: An interactionist theory of Indigenous cultures*. New York: SUNY Press.
Papastergiadis, N. (2012). *Cosmopolitanism and culture*. Cambridge: Polity Press.
Peng, R.-Z., Zhu, C., & Wu, W.-P. (2020). Visualizing the knowledge domain of intercultural competence research: A bibliometric analysis. *International Journal of Intercultural Relations, 74*, 58–68.
Sude, Yuan, M., & Dervin, F. (2020). *Introduction to ethnic minority education in China: Policies and practices*. Singapore: Springer.
Xie, M. (Ed.). (2014). *The agon of interpretations: Towards a critical intercultural hermeneutics*. Toronto: Toronto University Press.
Yong, J. (2018). *Legends of the condor heroes*. London: MacLehose Press.

Part II
Dealing with paradoxes of interculturality

5 Towards a diversity of thoughts

This chapter is based on the argument that the broad field of intercultural communication education needs to infuse *diversities* in the way interculturality is problematised and dealt with, away from single dominant ideologies that make the notion too 'obvious to be true'. This also requires accepting that approaches to interculturality need to face their own contradictions and inconsistencies and to move away from discourses of things like 'rationality', 'logic' and 'objectivity'. Trying out new things must lead to arguing, revising, testing and trying again and again. This process is never-ending – like intercultur*ality*. I maintain that constant movements forward and to and fro (Dervin & R'boul, 2023), in discussions with other scholars, educators and students, can help us make this necessary shift (temporarily) sustainable. It is only when we stop exploring and wishing for more – feeling content with 'our' models and 'orders' – that interculturality becomes a monological, purposeless and ideologically 'airproof' notion. *The end of interculturality*. The fragments gathered here focus on identifying sources of diverse thoughts and treating them in ethical ways. The reader is urged to be ready to share, to listen to others, to ask questions, to be quiet (at times) and to look at themselves from a distance.

~ **Fragments IV** ~

[Accents]

> The very word *interculturality* speaks with different porous accents that can absorb but also ooze each other. This is why interculturality must be an apple of discord. The more we disagree, the better off she is. *The more diverse she becomes.*

[Alienation]

Bertold Brecht's (see Bial & Martin, 2000) *theory of alienation/estrangement* in theatre is another inspiration for interculturality as a subject of discourse. Based on a specific performance apparatus, Brecht wanted to unsettle the audience by creating in them a sense of resistance against the capitalist social order, thinking and assessing critically about ways of change. Strategies used by Brecht included presenting familiar contents in unusual ways so that the audience would not relate directly with the plot but would think profoundly about the play.

We should approach interculturality *alienly*.

[Breakdown]

To try to rip interculturality off us is just impossible. We cannot cut off from interculturality. It is always there in us, on top of us, besides us, outside us, between us and others, in the 'things' we hold . . . cutting off from it would mean *breakdown*.

When one reads about interculturality one can witness the ideological short-circuits that take place in the world. He believes that some short-circuits can be fixed.

[Busy]

His self is so occupied with ideas from selves and others – like everybody else. His head is filled with complex and simple dialogues about interculturality. Juggling between these dialogues is a rewarding challenge.

[Chopsticks]

Interculturality is like chopsticks – this 'sacred' couple is independent from each other, but both 'sticks' are needed to be functional. In China, newlyweds often get chopsticks as presents. In one Minzu 'ethnic' area of the country, when a man wants to marry, his mother brings chopsticks in a red box to the fiancée's family. No need for her to speak; the family knows what this means. On rare occasions chopsticks can be used separately – like interculturality, in 'real' life, research and education, we always need others. When the other is 'broken off' from our conversations, it is not about interculturality anymore.

[Cocoon]

Although he works on *interculturality*, he has a duty to explore what scholars say about other companion notions such as *global, transcultural, culturally-responsive* (e.g. Bourn, 2020; Kirshner & Kamberelis, 2021; Stembridge, 2019). At times he agrees with them, at other times he doesn't. But *he needs to know* what their ideologies are. He needs to enrich his own take on his preferred term. He needs to move out of his own ideological cocoon and to navigate from one cocoon to another, noting similarities and differences, coherence and incoherence, contradictions, etc.

[Considerate]

To be considerate (恕, shù) in Chinese means to refrain from imposing one's own preferences and aversions on others, i.e. to let them *consider by themselves*. He is not entitled to tell you what interculturality is and how it should be done – unless he warns you that what he says cannot be taken at face value and is probably very much Eurocentric with a dose of American and Chinese ideologemes.

We need a new language to talk about interculturality. Interculturality is too gnomic, obscure, impenetrable, unknowable. He feels stuck and unable to talk about her without reducing her to falseness and one-sidedness. Interculturality as *je ne sais quoi* (Jankélévitch, 2014).

[Continue]

Having to write about interculturality as *an ideal* today feels somewhat ineffective and discouraging.

- There is a war in Ukraine. We are all part of this war.
- COVID-19 has killed millions of people due to neglect, greediness, lies and selfishness.
- Geopolitical bashing.

But we need to continue.
Interculturality is composed of endless *as ifs*.

[Distance]

We must first look at interculturality from a distance.

70 *Dealing with paradoxes of interculturality*

When he uses inverted commas to refer to 'intercultural' things that he does or to other entities, he takes a distance from them. By dropping the commas, he makes it more real; he shows that he accepts this distance. *He removes the distance somehow.*

M. Abramovic (2018, p. 75) said about her performance on the Great Wall of China with her former lover: "this is an encounter of our separation" – they separated after months of walking, each from a different direction of the Wall. He often views interculturality as necessary "encounters of our separation".

[Diversities]

Title of a book: *Intercultural Competence in Diverse Contexts*. Is any context *non-diverse*, where everybody is alike, indistinguishable, identical? Can two humans be so similar?

Different . . . different . . . different . . .
Monotonous
Different-similar-different-different-similar-diff . . .-si . . .-similar-different-diff . . .
Exhilarating.

Having seen bamboo in Asia and Europe, he never realised that there were different kinds until he saw a list of different 'bamboo families'. For him bamboo had just always been 'bamboo'. Some categories: *The stem-oriented* type (e.g. Huang Wen bamboo, black bamboo); *the leaf-oriented varieties* (e.g. Sasa fortunei, tranguillans f. shiro) and *the posture-oriented kinds* (e.g. arrow bamboo, Pseudosasa japonica). Curious about their differences, he goes to a 'bamboo park'. He cannot really see the difference, except maybe in terms of size. His blindness to this diversity is like the blindness to different ways of conceptualising and engaging with interculturality. *We must train our eyes and senses.*

Interculturality abounds so we must be ready to deal with multiplicity at all times.

Interculturality is a protean idea. Interculturality is the absence of form par excellence. *Interculturality is* the limitless, ultimateless, *to borrow concepts from Anaximander (Rovelli, 2023) and Zhuangzi (2022). Interculturality is not a single stone! (stone is from Greek for* monolith).

There are many terms in Chinese to describe the taste of tea, using 韵 (yun), which means rhyme, rhythm, charm and beauty (Zhang, 2021). For example, *throat yun* refers to a sweet lingering sensation in the throat after drinking tea. All these different sensations related to tea are like different flavours one might experience while engaging with the idea of interculturality from *authentically* global perspectives.

Contradictions and unpredictability as criteria for 'good' interculturality. The end of *intercultural competence*?

[Elastic]

> The definition of interculturality should be elastic and plastic and be moulded into an uncountable number of shapes. Let people dream interculturality together the way they want her to be.

Interculturality has no agenda. *Who knows where she is going?* Interculturality moves along arrhythmic leaps and bounds – *how to catch her? Can she be 'caught'?*

Interculturality has an atomic quality. She can mean so many different things. Interculturality resists formal systems. Interculturality should not be thought of in terms of well-developed doctrines but in changing cloudy forms.

Interculturality refuses to be corralled into a systematic order. Interculturality asks us not to get too involved in her messy outlook. She urges us to be patient and modest. Interculturality is a chimera – a mythical fire-breathing monster with a lion's head, a goat's body and a serpent's tail. In other words: *A fantasy!*

We should work on interculturality like shamans: Try to link up 'our' world with other worlds.

[Energy]

> In Chinese 氧气 (yang qi) refers to 'the energy of the West', *to shine like the West*, 'Western style' qi. How about we try other kinds of qi in research on interculturality?

[Ethics]

> Whatever interculturality is and whatever she aims for, what is certain is that she is every single being's responsibility. No one can close their eyes and pretend not to be part of her or affected by her.

There is some kind of moral push to use certain theories and perspectives of interculturality that would deserve to be undone.

If there is one important ethical aspect of interculturality, it is to open up to other ways of thinking and problematising the notion. *What does my neighbour think about her? How can we reconcile the way we understand her together?* These are the real and only problems of ethics.

[Fiction]

The older he gets, the more he is appreciative of the complexities and realities of fiction compared to the (sometimes) simplifying and tedious simplicity of research on interculturality. Fiction and philosophy feel so much richer ideologically. Scientific discourses on interculturality appear to be prosaic at times compared to what things like fiction or the cinema have to say about her. As a researcher, reading fiction and philosophy could allow stepping outside the (limited) ideological framework(s) of research.

[Fisheye camera]

Any view on interculturality is an anamorphosis, a perspective in the arts that gives a distorted image of the subject in a picture – e.g. reflecting them in a curved mirror. Research on interculturality should thus be like a fisheye camera, with a viewing angle of panoramic 360 degrees. We can look in all directions to grasp all the diversity of thoughts we can and to confront them with each other. *Interculturality can open to all directions at once.*

[Fragments]

Interculturality is always in fragments:

- Interaction   I am *in-between* voices/noises about interculturality
- Languages   I am *in-between* (forms) of languages when I interact around interculturality
- Ideologies   I am *crossed* and *torn apart* by multiple ideologies of interculturality
- Life experiences   I *confront* my life experiences with multifaceted discourses of interculturality

Interculturality is always *a snapshot of a snapshot of a snapshot of a snapshot.*[1] . . The dialectic between the fragment and the whole: That's what really matters for interculturality.

[Google]

Knowledge about interculturality should be like Google before it became this 'big data' machine that can retrieve precise information instantly. In the past there was something 'embryonic' in the way it provided information – like the way we should enter intercultural encounters.

Believing that one knows everything about the other, about the very notion of interculturality, is counterproductive. *Hesitation, 'slow' changeable knowledge, fuzzy images needed.*

[Harmony]

Aim for *Datong* (universal harmony)! *But we never will achieve it* . . . Harmony is about balancing otherness with otherness. It refutes sameness. Harmony is like interculturality – we must work at it lifelong.

When we do interculturality, we *weave together* "a tangled web" (Scott, 1894, p. 112).

Interculturality must be a drama/comedy of verbal seesaw. Interculturality is always a transition so we cannot get hold of her. *Transitionality* is thus a synonym for interculturality. Between *there is* and *there will be*, *between them* but also *them together*.

[Haunting]

Years of looking for interculturality. She is with him all the time. *But who is she? Why is she haunting him?* Sometimes he wishes she'd left him alone.

[Humanity]

At some water resort in China in 2018, a Beluga and Sea Lion are made to perform tricks that mimic the human (shake heads, clap, put a hat on . . .). No real interculturality here; just human behaviours. Anyone would identify with what they perform. The audience is enthusiastic and cheers every time they recognise aspects of their humanness in the animals. Interestingly, while re-reading Bergson's (1900/1985, p. 3) *The Laughter*, he notes that the philosopher made a similar remark about an animal entertaining people at a circus. When we perform *being intercultural* – meaning here: try to behave like (the)(each) other in somewhat stereotypical ways – we are just like the Beluga and Sea Lion. *Entertainers* at the mercy of other humans.

Please remember our humanity, hence our diversity! Interculturality is about *humans*, not *cultures*.

Interculturality both plagiarises and transforms the complexities of the world and humanity.

[Isonomy]

Isonomy needed in research on interculturality: The equality of all before the law; no one orders anyone about what she is and how to 'do' her. Interculturality as a *placebo* only according to its etymology: *I shall be acceptable or pleasing!*

[Jewel]

Often the way he 'reads' art and music reminds him of how little scholarship on interculturality can appeal to him or stimulate him. But when he finds a jewel, *it dazzles him*. Interculturality should be a miracle – *miraculum* in Latin: A subject of wonder. Not a mere subject of *automatisms*.

[Life]

Life must inspire scholars and educators. We cannot ignore it and speak of interculturality as if she were a cold, distant subject.

There is no need to hide behind grand theories, aggrandised concepts and notions, *guruesque* figures. Interculturality pushes us to explore and reveal ourselves and others. She does not call for objectivisation but treatment as a 'living thing'.
Interculturality is life. Life is interculturality.
Interculturality does not exist – only in a fluid uncontrollable form. This is why we cannot map her out, since:

- This would assume that we can talk about her together in the same way;
- As a subject of research, she is so multifaceted globally that it would not even be possible to register all the scholars, educators and individuals who deal with her;
- *Interculturality* is just a word. The realities out there are far too complex. *LIFE*.

He uses the word *reality* in the plural in this book, agreeing with Woolf (1998, p. 83):

It [reality] would seem to be something very erratic, very undependable – now to be found in a dusty road, now in a scrap of newspaper in the street, now a daffodil in the sun. It lights up a group in a room and stamps some casual saying. It overwhelms one walking home beneath the stars and makes the silent world more real than the world of speech. . . . Sometimes, too, it seems to dwell in shapes too far away for us to discern what their nature is.

[Love]

He heard in a video of young kids defining *love*: "Love is when you love somebody, and it's when you love somebody and it's really when you love somebody". Replace *love* with *interculturality*.

[Metaphors]

A metaphor is an act of interculturality, *a bridge to the other*. We also need counter-metaphors, going back and forth. Creating metaphors with the other is an interesting entry into interculturality. A student of his uses the metaphor of *the sky* to describe the complexities of interculturality. The student reminds him that clouds change shapes and colours all the time – like words to describe interculturality – and that one cannot always predict the weather as it is changeable – *like interculturality*.

[Mottoes]

Looking at many countries' mottoes one notices a lot of overlaps, similarities and 'copycatting'. Some include *'God'*, others *liberty, freedom* . . . Always approach a country by looking at their symbols – *they always reveal interculturality first and foremost*. We are different and similar. *Differilitude* (Dervin, 2022).

[Music]

The pleasure of discovering new perspectives from art, music, fiction, that can push us to think further about interculturality. When one is listening to one's favourite piece of music on a player and another piece starts playing suddenly, and although one is not so fond of it at first, one discovers that, in fact, it can be quite pleasing after a while. Interculturality as a subject of research and education is the same. We may not like the way others formulate her at first but with patience, modesty and honesty, we might start appreciating her and building upon/from her with them.

[Navigate]

In Chinese, chemistry means *the study of movement and change*. A perfect definition for what we 'do' with interculturality.

He is navigating between one author and another, one composer to another, one artist to another; looking for something, chasing after something (new). He feels that there is urgency, but he doesn't know what he is looking for and/or why it really matters.

Interculturality could be about the following continua (in alphabetical order):

- brevity < . . . > thoroughness
- confrontation < . . . > coexistence
- estrangement < . . . > intimacy
- flexibility < . . . > rigor
- opposition < . . . > symbiosis
- roughness < . . . > precision
- struggle < . . . > harmony.

Interculturality cannot but be *either/or*.

Inter- and *intra-* are two sides of the same coin. We always need to create opposites. But what we mean by *intracultural* is unclear, as if one could divide the indivisible.

A huiwen (回文词) from the Song Dynasty (960–1279) is a type of Chinese poem that is palindromic, reversible and circular (Métail, 2017). It has no end, no beginning, but (temporary) *beginnings* and *ends*. One can pick any word from the poem and read it in any direction. A word found in huiwen is always the potential beginning of a new poem. Thousands of poems can then appear and be read endlessly. *Hui* means *back, to return, to revolve, to curve, to cycle*. A perfect metaphor for interculturality, which has no direction; neither beginning nor end (Dervin, 2022). A great metaphor for the need to read her in diverse ways. *All we can do is navigate her waters aimlessly*. An interculturalist is thus someone who allows their mind to float and to be calm and relaxed about the contradictions they experience. We must sleepwalk through intercultural education and research. There is no direction. Let intuition guide us.

[Objects]

Can only the human be intercultural? Can an object also *be*? Yes, they are intercultural in our eyes; they are there, they are part of our encounters. But we will never find out if they consider what we do together *intercultural* (Itkonen & Dervin, 2017). Only human beings care about labelling.

[Palimpsest]

Interculturality is a palimpsest *par excellence* (from Greek *palimpsestos* for *scraped again*). She has layers and layers of meanings and connotations under the surface . . . Interculturality is a garden-like expansion. When we speak of interculturality, often, *signifieds* and *signifiers* refuse to conjoin.

In the end, every perspective of interculturality is like a hall of mirrors; warped, distorted versions.

Could *interculturalising interculturality* contribute to the democratisation of intercultural knowledge – *to twist a Eurocentric idea*?

[Past]

Looking at 'our' past is an intercultural experience. We might also misread it with 'our' contemporary ideological lenses. We need to diversify the way history is perceived.

[Person]

Behind an ideology – this automaton way of speaking about something or spreading orders, commands – there is always a real person or a group of persons. Always try to identify who they are (in most cases, we can't know).

Interculturality is about becoming a person with multiple masks with others. It is about the *persona*. Interculturality consists of encounters with selves by way of alterity.

[(We are all) researchers]

If we just open our eyes and look around, we notice that we are in fact all researchers and specialists of interculturality. Every time we experience her, we try to make sense of her, we try to rethink her and ponder over her – alone with ourselves and/or with others. That's why we need to listen to others, not just 'hear' them.

[Riot]

Interculturality is a riot of polysemy (a diversity of thoughts!) which leads him to contradict himself. Is he thus 'good' at interculturality? *Contradictions are the key!*

[Share and care]

Akinboye Akinbiyi's (2011) *prêt-à-partager* is stimulating for interculturality as a subject of research and education. We must be ready to listen to others, to ask questions, to (re-)negotiate answers but also to accept that we don't know, to be quiet and to look at ourselves from a distance in the mirrors of the other. *Ready-to-share. Prêt-à-partager* instead of Byram's (1997) *savoirs*. That's all we need for interculturality, he feels.

Pay attention to the humility of the unnoticed in the way interculturality is discussed globally.

[Their]

Maybe we should ask students what they would want us to do with interculturality. He has tried. It takes time for them to trust him enough to share what they would want to learn and experience. Once trust is established, we can create curricula, learning outcomes and teaching content *together*. *Our* interculturality.

[To be]

Interculturality is neither good nor bad. *It just is*. Doing interculturality is using keys to who we are together.

[Turmoil]

Doing interculturality is experiencing *turmoil* – a word assumed to come from French for a *mill hopper*, in reference to the latter's constant motion to and fro. Interculturality follows the same frenzied movements.

[Understand]

Speaking to 'non-scholars' about interculturality (people on the streets, writers, artists, musicians) met randomly reminds him that we all aim one way or another for the same good: To understand and explain who we are (together). He often finds such conversations to be most inspiring. For Borges (in Alifano & Domec, 1984, p. 15): "All that happens to us, including our humiliations, our misfortunes, our embarrassments, all is given to us as raw material, as clay, so that we may shape our art".

During the pandemic, and especially in moments of crisis such as lockdowns across the globe, people constantly performed 'discourse analyses' of what authorities were saying, trying to make sense of the jargon used, the neologisms and the 'orders'. For example, a Chinese netizen called 拆台师 ('*demolutionist*', the one who tears down), often published about the use of new phrases and terms introduced by the authorities to talk about the restrictions for the pandemic. In France, Macron's use of a consulting cabinet which created a certain number of (discursive) 'nudges' to protect people during lockdowns was also analysed by people. These forms of 'folk discourse analysis' are important and we should listen to them when it comes to how people perceive interculturality and how she is 'done'.

After a discussion with a Chinese colleague about B. Anderson's *Imagined Communities* (2016), he realised the way they had perceived the consequences of these communities differently. For him, they have always led to the worst woes of the 21st century: *Ethnocentrism, wars, genocides, conflicts, cruelty*. For them: *Togetherness, celebrating unity*.

[Us]

Interculturality is within us, even before we try to spot her.

He is never alone when he thinks about interculturality. Hundreds of different heads are with him. There is still enough space for many more heads.

Interculturality has (always) been, is and will always be *our* destiny. No one can escape from her.

[Voices]

Only when he engages with others' voices does he get inspired. Reading and talking to students have saved him from fatigue over the past years. Research on interculturality as *Gesamt Kunstwerke*: a synthesis of the arts, a synthesis of different kinds of knowledge, interdisciplinarity *par excellence* – gleaning through fields, subfields, the arts, philosophy and the everyday.

Tonality (for 'us' interculturalists: dominating Western ideologies of interculturality) is often opposed to *atonality* (e.g. revising these ideologies critically) in music (see Dervin & Yuan, 2022). Schoenberg (2003) opposes them to *pantonality* or giving equal value to all tones in music. In interculturality this would mean listening to every single one of us in research and education. *A beautiful ideal.* However, this represents possibly an impossibility in an English-dominated world of research.

[Writing]

> As a researcher-writer-lecturer-intellectual working on interculturality, he has many identities from the cold, impersonal, dogmatic EU report writer to the square, limited research article (co-)writer; from the liberated, creative book writer to the passionate but tired PhD report writer. These all enrich his thoughts about interculturality and although some of these positions are more tedious than others, they form together the complex menagerie of voices that are out there for the world to enjoy, appreciate, despise and reject.

Stereotypical writing about interculturality, through the use of unproblematised ready-mades such as 'non-essentialism', claims of care for 'social justice' and 'democracy', leads to illusions and degradation of the complexities of the notion.

Writing about interculturality is his main tool in researching her. Navigating through thoughts, definitions, contradictions, disagreements is what we need to deal with her.

A book is only written through the experiences of other people and through the voices we have heard from them.

The process of writing is just like the process of making art. Sometimes it is terrific and original, sometimes it is dull and meaningless – at least for the one producing the writing! Art is a good substitute and companion for writing about interculturality.

He cares about his readers, but he does not wish to impose anything on them. He wants us to take each other by the hand and move forward and backward and in all directions together. If a reader is confused about what he writes and decides to step out, it is their decision to do so. *Caring is not imposing.*

We would need phatics such as *isn't it?, right?* to negotiate better 'communion' with others when we write about interculturality. We need an illusion of dialogue with our readers – not just the sempiternal one-way dialogue between a writer and a reader. While he writes about interculturality he'd like to know what his readers think, what they make of what he writes and how, through their dialogues, he could change. (Note: *remember your readers!*).

Writing about interculturality must be like a sizeable extended family; one book grows from and into another. *A book is never the end.*

~ Interthinking ~

Start by reflecting on the very word *diversity* in the English language. Check its etymology. Do an archaeology of its changing meanings and applications throughout history. What does it mean today? What does it refer to in daily life, economic-political discourses, education, research, business, etc.? If you have access to different forms of 'Englishes' in different parts of the world, observe the nuances one might attach to the word. Then do the same exercise with diversity in other languages that you might know. Is the word avoided in certain languages or is it substituted by another term? From there, problematise for yourself what a diversity of thoughts might refer to for interculturality in research and education. What aspects might be covered by *diversity*?

Now read through the following questions and try to provide some answers. You can always come back to them at a later stage if you still need time to formulate your answers.

+ How much do you know about *global, transcultural* and *culturally-responsive* education? What differences and similarities do they seem to share with intercultural education?
+ How often have you tried to reconnect your own views on interculturality with your colleagues, teachers or other students? In other words, have you been able to change your mind genuinely about aspects of interculturality through engaging with others? Have you had major disagreements? Why?
+ What do you make of my claim in one of the fragments that "reading fiction and philosophy allows stepping outside the (limited) ideological framework(s) of research"? Has this been your experience? How often do you 'consult' e.g. fiction for inspiration?
+ I use the concept of *ideology* many times in the book. How would you define it at this stage? And what are the potential connections between awareness of ideologies and a diversity of thoughts in intercultural research and education?
+ Do you consciously "pay attention to the humility of the 'unnoticed' in the way interculturality is discussed globally"? How? Who? And why? What have you learnt from them (e.g. some scholars from the 'Global South')?
+ In a fragment, I describe my multiple identities as a researcher-writer-lecturer-intellectual in terms of writing. Review the different writing or

speaking activities in which you are involved: *Who are you in this 'forest' of selves (and others!)?*

And to finish, a few excerpts from the fragments for you to prepare for the next chapter, which deals with criticality (of criticality):

> "Interculturality is composed of endless *as ifs*".
> "Interculturality should not be thought of in terms of well-developed doctrines but as changing cloudy forms".
> "Interculturality must be a drama/comedy of verbal seesaw".
> "Interculturality cannot but be *either/or*".

Note

1 The repetition of this word was suggested by Andreas Jacobsson in one of our conversations. A great reminder of the 'spiral-like' in discourses of interculturality.

References

Abramovic, M. (2018). *Marina Abramovic: Writings 1960–2014*. Köln: Walther König.

Akinbiyi, A. (2011). *Pret-a-Partager: Transcultural exchange in art, fashion and sports*. Wien: Verlag Fur Moderne Kunst.

Alifano, R., & Domecq, B. (1984). *Twenty-four conversations with Borges: Including a selection of poems: Interviews, 1981–1983*. New York: Lascaux Publishers.

Anderson, B. (2016). *Imagined communities. Reflections on the origin and spread of nationalism*. London: Verso.

Bergson, H. (1985). *Le rire*. Paris: PUF. (Original work published 1900)

Bial, H., & Martin, C. (Eds.). (2000). *Brecht sourcebook*. London: Routledge.

Bourn, D. (Ed.). (2020). *The Bloomsbury handbook of global education and learning*. London: Bloomsbury.

Byram, M. (1997). *Teaching and assessing intercultural communicative competence*. Clevedon: Multilingual Matters.

Dervin, F. (2022). *Interculturality in fragments: A reflexive approach*. Singapore: Springer.

Dervin, F., & R'boul, H. (2023). *Through the looking-glass of interculturality: Autocritiques*. Singapore: Springer.

Dervin, F., & Yuan, M. (2022). Political ideology and atonality in language and intercultural education: A rejoinder to 'Between professionalism and political engagement in foreign language teaching practice' by Claire Kramsch. *Journal of Applied Linguistics and Professional Practice, 16*(3), 31–45.

Itkonen, T., & Dervin, F. (Eds.). (2017). *Silent partners in multicultural education*. Charlotte, NC: IAP.

Jankélévitch, V. (2014). *Le Je-ne-sais-quoi et le Presque-rien. La Manière et l'Occasion*. Paris: Le Seuil.
Kirshner, J., & Kamberelis, G. (2021). *Decolonizing transcultural teacher education through participatory action research: Dialogue, culture, and identity*. London: Routledge.
Métail, M. (2017). *Wild Geese returning: Chinese reversible poems*. New York: New York Review Books.
Rovelli, C. (2023). *Anaximander: And the birth of science*. New York: Riverhead Books.
Schoenberg, A. (2003). *A Schoenberg reader* (Ed. J. Auner). New Haven, CT and London: Yale University Press.
Scott, W. (1894). *The complete poetical works of Sir Walter Scott*. Boston, MA: Thomas Crowell.
Stembridge, A. (2019). *Culturally responsive education in the classroom: An equity framework for pedagogy*. London: Routledge.
Woolf, V. (1998). *The waves*. Oxford: Oxford University Press.
Zhang, J. (2021). "A sense of life": The abstruse language of taste in Chinese culture. *Food, Culture & Society*. https://doi.org/10.1080/15528014.2021.1971437
Zhuangzi. (2022). 莊子. *Chinese Text Project*. https://ctext.org/zhuangzi

6 Criticality (of criticality)

The ideas of criticality, critical thinking and the like are now omnipresent in research on interculturality and many claims of one being 'critical' are made constantly in the literature: *One must be critical to be credible*. But what being critical in this context actually means and entails seems to be polysemous and multifaceted.

Many book titles contain the word 'critical'. I am limiting the following short discussion to books published in English in recent years[1] – I am aware that books that do not contain the word in their titles might also be classified as 'critical', but to get a sense of what has been explicitly named 'critical' I am offering this short review. Only one book series published by Peter Lang and co-edited by Nakayama and Calafell has the word in its title: *Critical Intercultural Communication Studies*. At the time of writing, 29 volumes had been published. The book series description on the publisher's website explains (www.peterlang.com/series/cics):

> This series will interrogate – from a critical perspective – the role of communication in intercultural contact, in both domestic and international contexts. Through attentiveness to the complexities of power relations in intercultural communication, this series is open to studies in key areas such as postcolonialism, transnationalism, critical race theory, queer diaspora studies, and critical feminist approaches as they relate to intercultural communication.

I note the use of 'a critical perspective' in the singular in this quote, a (preferred?) focus on 'power relations', and a list of 'critical' paradigms/perspectives as entries into the issue of intercultural communication.

Books containing the very word *critical* include (in chronological order):

Intercultural Communication: A Critical Introduction (Piller, 2011)
The Handbook of Critical Intercultural Communication (eds. Nakayama & Halualani, 2012)

DOI: 10.4324/9781003371052-8
This chapter has been made available under a CC-BY-NC-ND 4.0 license.

The Agon of Interpretations: Towards a Critical Intercultural Hermeneutics (ed. Xie, 2014)
The Critical Turn in Language and Intercultural Communication pedagogy: Theory, Research and Practice (eds. Dasli & Díaz, 2016)
Intercultural Communication: Critical Approaches and Future Challenges (Ferri, 2018)
The Discourse of Special Populations: Critical Intercultural Communication Pedagogy and Practice (Atay, 2019)
Postcolonial Turn and Geopolitical Uncertainty: Transnational Critical Intercultural Communication pedagogy (eds. Atay & Chen, 2020)
Glocal Languages and Critical Intercultural Awareness: The South Answers Back (eds. Guilherme & Menezes de Souza, 2020)
Critical Intercultural Communication Pedagogy (eds. Atay & Toyosaki, 2020)
Teaching Social Justice: Critical Tools for the Intercultural Communication Classroom (Lawless & Chen, 2021)
Language and Intercultural Communication in Tourism: Critical perspectives (eds. Sharma & Gao, 2021)
Teacher Education for Critical and Reflexive Interculturality (Dervin & Jacobsson, 2021)
Intercultural management: Concepts, Practice, Critical Reflection (Holtbrugge, 2022)
Critical Intercultural Pedagogy for Difficult Times: Conflict, Crisis, and Creativity (Holmes & Corbett, 2022).

These are all the book titles that I was able to retrieve in English (I apologise to colleagues whose book might be missing from the list). The books are from the (sub-)fields of business, communication, language education, pedagogy, philosophy, teacher education, tourism and represent a good range of (sub-)fields interested in interculturality. The following uses of the word *critical* are noted:

- Critical applies to *interculturality directly* (critical and reflexive interculturality);
- Critical is included in *the name of a '(sub-)field'* (critical intercultural communication, pedagogy, transnational critical intercultural communication pedagogy, critical intercultural hermeneutics);
- Critical refers to a 'method' (introduction, perspectives, tools, turn);
- Critical is attached to a concept (reflection, intercultural awareness).

Finally, I note that the following topics 'orbit' around the word critical (in alphabetical order): conflict/crisis/creativity, language, practice, reflexivity, social justice, theory. Two books seem to adopt a 'decolonial' perspective.

86 *Dealing with paradoxes of interculturality*

What seems to be missing in the proposed 'critical' perspectives from this selection of books (again: We need to look deeper into research articles and chapters), is what I call 'criticality of criticality'. Adopting critical perspectives whereby we observe what others (research participants, scholars, educators, decision-makers) do; digging into their agendas and ideologies; collecting their biases and stereotypes; comparing what they say and do to others; noting problems and proposing solutions or making recommendations, is *noble* and *praiseworthy* – I have been doing it for decades. However, what seems to be missing in most 'critical' research on interculturality is the use of a 'looking-glass', i.e. to look at oneself as a scholar, an educator, a student, from a distance. In Murdoch's (2002, p. 10) *Henry and Cato*, the author writes: "One should go easy on smashing other people's lies. Better to concentrate on one's own". This is what I call criticality of criticality – being critical of what we construct as being critical. Without this constant process of observing oneself being critical towards others, we fall into the trap of ideological blindness, egocentrism or – *criticentrism* – placing one's criticality in the centre, ignoring the need to decenter that criticality too. 双管齐下 (shuāngguǎnqíxià) in Chinese could translate as *painting a picture with two brushes at the same time*. Criticality of criticality corresponds to the same process: I keep one eye and ear open to the world around me while my other eye and ear watch over this process. Since interculturality cannot but be ideological, *we need to watch ourselves watching others*.

~ Fragments V ~

[China]

Someone he hasn't met for a long time finds that he has changed a lot since the last time they interacted – before the 2020-... pandemic. "What happened"?, they inquire. He replies: *Staying at home, I have had the time to reconsider my memories and fantasies of China – and thus of myself.*

[Criticality]

'Critical' as a good narrative.
A course on critical thinking in China proposes to help students learn to think 'logically'. He wonders what that could mean.
Criticality of claims of criticality needed.
Being critical is, of course, praiseworthy. Activism for e.g. social justice, equality and decolonialism in research and education is honourable. However, any form of criticality and activism that does not take

into account the 'violence' represented by language, which cannot but be ideological and polysemic across forms of languages, entails biting one's tail.

Putting criticality on the table is often a way to close the door to potential discussions. It is like saying: *You cannot defeat me. I am critical thus I am right. I cannot be a bad person.* We need modest criticality.

Claims of criticality can camouflage 'a-criticality'. If one is critical, one remains silent about being critical – *and just do it. The illusion of critical thinking.* It seems to him that the more we claim to be doing it, the more 'protected' we feel we are. Protected against what *is, however, a mystery.* A lot of the critical thinking that we claim to be doing is in fact a-critical, a travesty, an illusion . . .

The a-critical is an omnipresent figure in research on interculturality, who is never named as such but imagined. In any case, it is never *me*. By using the word *critical* in our work, we are disenfranchised from being considered as a member of this category. *Or are we?*

Critical interculturality is often a mask. Claims of criticality help continue dominating the world of thoughts. We can decide how people talk (how they should not), what they can talk about (or not) and thus control the voices that get heard. Disruptive voices are silenced by the impossibility of criticising the established criticality. For example, non-essentialism, as an ideal, 'blocks the way' for any other possible perspective on interculturality. *It has to be beyond the essence.* The real question here being*: Can we really do this?*

Litanies instead of criticalities. Criticalities instead of litanies.

What is the 'critical' of criticality in relation to interculturality in education today?

- The clearly *Political* – the political with a capital P. He is thinking of the ideas of 'democratic culture' and 'intercultural citizenship' from Europe, which aim to promote ideologies such as (European?) democracy, human rights . . .
- The clearly *Political mistaken for being a critical scientific perspective*, used a-politically – e.g. the Political as pedagogy.
- Critical perspectives that are politically oriented based on the values of e.g. *social justice, equality and equity, anti-discrimination* – these terms, being elastic, can be used either as empty signifiers or as embedded modifiers in different economic-political contexts.
- Critical perspectives that are *not clearly politically engaged but positioned* in openly ideologically idealistic perspectives such as non-essentialism, non-culturalism, decoloniality.
- Emerging critical perspectives based on *the critical ideologies* of e.g. postcolonial and queer studies.

What is missing are critical perspectives that look at themselves from outside by utilising their own frameworks to analyse themselves and by focusing on politics of languaging interculturality (i.e. creating discourses around interculturality in different forms of languages).

One-sided criticality turns research into potential political propaganda. A certain compulsion towards constant self-questioning and reassessment of our work is what an interculturalist needs – in research and education.

"I argue that" often seems to mean "I just repeat dominating 'critical' views (like litanies)". By rehearsing the same words borrowed from the powerful, we endanger our own criticality. The automatism they create limits the impact of our critique. We must move beyond systems of critiques anchored in such ways that they imprison us in one-sided/a-critical criticality.

Could and *might* are intercultural – opening up the *inter-*. *Must* and *should* work against interculturality, closing the door to the *inter-*. He has used a lot of *musts* and *shoulds* in this book. Is he not interculturally-friendly?

We must criticise *all* thoughts, otherwise we give the impression that they are not strong enough. Refusing to criticise an idea because it comes from the 'Global South' is patronising. This idea can (obviously) stand up and (re-)negotiate criticisms too.

For Barthes (1984), criticality is about "mettre en crise le langage" – to create a crisis within language. *To create crises within and out of language.* These crises we must observe and act upon in intercultural research.

Discard the ones we admire. Move forward.

Do not varnish knowledge of interculturality. It should be roughened, scuffed up.

A reminder to self: *Be critical of your own criticality of criticality!* Stop performing criticality! Be critical of everything. Be comfortable with contradictions (reminder to self).

[Discard]

Let's clean up our brains from time to time. Sometimes we should just forget concepts, ideas and thinkers. *He will appear as a nihilist.*

He doesn't write for recognition. His words can be discarded. It does not matter.

In order to deal with interculturality we must be experts in not owning concepts, ideas or theories. Sentimentalism to be banished.

[Ethnic]

A reminder: The word *ethnic* in English first referred to people who did not belong to the Jewish or Christian faiths. A religious-centric word that has spread to other corners of the world. Many of us avoid discussing religion, how about thinking twice before using the word 'ethnic'?

[Evils]

How many of those who make us feel guilty about inequalities and social injustice in research do not actually contribute to the *evils* that they describe in-/directly? He sees this scholar writing against the foes of neoliberalism in education – but he cannot help noticing how much they have benefitted from it to be where they are.

[Faces]

Why do faces always pop up in his art, even when he doesn't draw people? His anthropocentric obsession. *I, you, they*. Interculturality as a human 'thing' only.

[Fogainsting]

Fogainsting – a neologism for describing the interrelations between *being for* and *against* something or someone. The border between these two is not always discernible as far as interculturality is concerned.

[Ideology]

Ideology is always the other. *I am the un-ideological* par excellence – *the flexible, the liberal, the latitudinarian, the undoctrinaire*. Revise.

[Inertia]

Inertia of intercultural research: recycling ideas and ideologies, pretending to be 'more' critical, using different terms for rehearsing the same.

Interculturalising interculturality may not be the right move because of the polysemy of the very notion. What is, in the end, this 'thing' to interculturalise? Whose? Does it exist in such an easily describable and packageable format that this would even be possible? And who decides on the interculturalising process? Could this too easily turn into another false move to take control of knowledge production?

[(The) intellectual]

Being a scholar does not mean that one should be popular, looking for fame or pleasing others. The scholar should aim to disrupt, to displease, to help rethink, to note the 'disturbable'. *Popularity is weakness.*

We must apply our own intercultural principles to ourselves. Whatever they may be.

When we write about interculturality, we cannot but internalise ourselves in the subject. We always see ourselves in our research; we cannot close our eyes and pretend that we don't see our reflection. How much of what we say and theorise about interculturality also has to do with our own uncertainty and fear?

Like the artist E. L. Kirchner (1880–1938) who insisted on making frames for his art by himself, we should work out temporary frames for every idea that we produce about interculturality, to delimit clearly what we *really* want to say . . . not to ensnare them but to make sure that we know why we are promoting specific ideas at moment X. *Frameless assertions can fool us.*

The scholar's voice is desired not always because of what they say but because of what they represent and 'do' to our *own identity* as listeners and readers – e.g. I have met them *physically* at a conference; I have heard them speak, *I was there. Ideas first!*

For Anton Webern (cited in Fisk, 1997, p. 292), no need to write music entirely by ear. Ears will always guide us all right, but we must know *why* we are writing music and in specific ways. Maybe that is also the real question for interculturality: *why are we writing about it?*

[Intolerance]

He understood what *intolerance* really meant by reading what many of us researchers have to say about interculturality in education. Note, for example, how the so-called 'culturalist' is now considered as a 'pariah'. In some years, the 'non-culturalist' will be thought of as a 'relic'.

[-isms]

Working on interculturality without -isms in mind: *A cul-de-sac?*

Interculturalising interculturality is *still* not doing *interculturalising anything* since it *still* tends to use contestable ideologies of interculturality from the West (*still*). *Interculturalising interculturality-ism.*

Barthes (2002, p. 91) suggests putting small Japanese bell pins on what we say as a trigger warning for when we fall into *-isms* (any -ism!). For interculturality, this would mean that when we see certain words like *culture, decolonial, democracy, non-essentialism*, we beware.

The same applies to modals such as *must* and *should* in discourses of interculturality: Small bell pins needed to remind us to think twice before imposing.

[Mirror]

> Interculturality must be a mirror of transformation – *not imitation*. Transformation here does not necessarily mean *achievement*.

[Money]

> While watching an old interview from an American TV channel, he realises that, to announce the ad break, the presenter says, "and now we need to pay some bills. We'll be right back!". How he wishes we were so direct about 'money' issues in intercultural research and education because, at the end of the day, everything that we do has to do with *money* when it comes to interculturality – like it or not!

Seems to be so hard to reflect on the real issues in interculturality: *Money* and *the political!* What is that social injustice that we are talking about in the 'West'? It all comes down to money . . . money is at the centre of all these evils that we put on the table: Racism, discrimination, inequality, etc. One can notice clear interference from the market in the way interculturality is dealt with in research and education, but we keep quiet about it.

'Conflicts' can be explained by culture, politics, one's own (perceived) superiority. *However, what about the role of economics in conflicts?*

At a supermarket, the way goods are presented has to do with how much a company will have paid a premium to get promoted to the most privileged place on shelves and gondolas – at the eye-level shelving space, *the prime space*. This is referred to as *shelf impact*. The lower or the higher the position (usually cheaper products, less famous brands, items for children), the less attention they will attract. Research on interculturality does the same: We all get to see the most popular and privileged 'brands' (the best-selling discourses, ideologies, concepts, promoted through premium payments of belonging to top universities with access to top international publishers and funding). We need to look up and to bend down to have access to other perspectives, which might not look so appealing at first – different discourses, 'cheap-looking' at first, 'incomprehensible', 'naïve', etc. – but with exploration and serious interest in them, we will discover new doors to knowledge of interculturality.

Models of intercultural competence fit very well with today's (plural) capitalist ideology: Let's save money by making things 'simpler' and organised, and by giving them the illusion that they are in control – and by letting the 'powerful' control them. They don't mean to help us as individuals but to help the system make use of us. *The market decides which idea about interculturality is the best, the strongest 'voice', the 'rightest' in research.*

A new research and teaching initiative is set up by universities in a European country and 'Africa', China and India. He receives a message from the organisers presenting their '*brand identity kit*' . . . Does this label reveal too much about some hidden agenda?

The 'Western' media obsession with the impact of the way China is dealing with COVID-19 on the world economy reveals what matters to them: *Money!* Discourses of democracy, freedom, human rights might just be shadow puppets.

Economic censorship – not allowing people to speak or to participate in discussions because of money inequalities – could be much worse than political censorship. Economic censorship is probably the most widespread form of censorship.

Capitalism always wins in the end, wherever.

[Musicalisation]

There is a need for the musicalisation of interculturality to undo the ritornellos in our heads and to thread and patch different pieces.

Conversation with a Chinese friend:

- (him) "Chinese first names usually have just one character. At least, for many of the people around me".
- (friend) "*Get out of your own surroundings and observe*. Probably as many will have first names with two characters".

[New]

Can we say anything about interculturality that has not yet been chewed on?

Conflict is a source of newness too.

He thought he was inventing something new about interculturality in the 2010s, but he was merely rehashing what some 'Western' anthropologists and sociologists had said. In the 1990s, he swallowed what European linguists and language educators claimed about interculturality, but the vast majority was just repeating what appeared to be (already old) banalities in other fields and in other parts of the world. After reading a recent paper by a novice scholar, he noticed that they were going through the same process, still the tendency to *copy-paste, to pastiche and patchwork.*

[Pioneers]

Considering the long history of interculturality, can we do anything pioneering about her today? Having looked into Ancient Chinese philosophy, his colleague is shocked to discover that a lot of what they had uttered could be useful to decipher interculturality today.

[Plant]

He saw a plant growing through the tarmac the other day. What a struggle it must have been! *But it did it.* That tarmac is the resistance to interculturalising interculturality. The plant gives hope. We must struggle on!

[Pride]

Pride is frustrating. It gives a feeling of achievement which has no place in research on interculturality. What is there to achieve in *this* world of 2022?
The only thing he is proud of is not to be proud of anything.

[Privilege]

If English is not one's first language, this is not necessarily a 'burden' or a 'negative thing'. Considering the complexity of the English language globally (its *glocality*), not being a so-called native speaker of English can be a safe and fluid position. One is not necessarily bound by specific local 'native' linguistic rules. *A privileged form of freedom that should be used for creativity and criticality!*

As someone who is privileged and part of the global elite, is he credible in his calls in this book?

[Refuse]

> Concepts are not meant to be chanted, rehearsed, litanised *but* criticised, opened up, operated on and discarded from time to time.

Writing, reading and publishing others' work about interculturality, there are moments when one must refuse: refuse certain ways of speaking, writing, showing off one's views, being intolerant of others' views on the notion.

[Risks]

> Research on interculturality must be *all-terrain* – ready for the unexpected; accepting of contradictions and inconsistencies; looking at oneself in the mirror.

[Side by side]

> He doesn't want followers, fans or even comrades in his work on interculturality. He just wants to move forward with/without others. *No one should follow*. Just walk side by side and struggle together, losing each other's sight in the process but still moving forward. Following can mean losing one's sense of directions. *Even alone, one is never by oneself in research on interculturality*.

"I don't read before I write, not to be influenced". But the whole world, others, our previous interactions, the books we have read, are always there when we write . . . we are *side-by-side*, one influencing the other (maybe) more than the other.

Interculturality should also be a silent dialogue with self – *a crowded solitary activity*. He wants to turn Barthes's (1977, p. 170) around: "What he listened to, what he could not keep from listening to, wherever he was, was the deafness of others to their own language: he heard them not hearing each other". We must listen to ourselves, not just hearing each other in intercultural research!

[Surprise]

> Any idea that does not surprise us should not be written down.

[Think]

> Ideas are too contagious. We do not always think for ourselves.

[Western scholars]

> Thinking about the current discussions around the divide between the Global North and the Global South: *What is the ultimate goal and for whom?* If it is just to describe the way 'they' are hierarchised and the multifaceted injustices that 'they' experience, we may not go anywhere – don't we already know that? *Action is all we need. Real action.*

As a privileged Western scholar, he must remind himself constantly that, while he is free to spread 'his' ideas about interculturality, millions of people are 'violenced' through ideas being imposed onto them.

~ Interthinking ~

Start this interthinking session by reflecting on the very idea of *criticality of criticality*. What does it mean to you? Is this something that you already do? Think about the books and articles that you have read about interculturality: do some of them present a perspective that you would categorise as criticality of criticality? How could it be practiced systematically in research and education?

Now it is time for questions about the content of the fragments:

+ How do you understand the idea of 'creating a crisis within language' (Barthes, 1984) to speak about interculturality? Can you think of concrete examples of how this could materialise in e.g. writing about interculturality? Speculate also about the potential benefits and drawbacks.
+ Let's go back to the idea of 'money', which I have argued repeatedly in the book is often 'avoided' and thus 'underground' in a lot of research on interculturality. Can you now try to think of concrete examples of how 'money' does influence interculturality in daily life and/or in research and education?
+ Read through one of the last articles or chapters that you have read and collect all instances where the author uses *should/must* and *could/must* (you can go back to the fragments in this book if you like). What do you notice? When do these modals appear and what are their functions? What do they tell us about what the author is doing?
+ Do you agree with me that not being a 'native speaker' of English is in fact an advantage in research on interculturality, since it means that one does not have to be 'stuck' in a limited number of meanings, connotations and 'flavours' of words? If you are multilingual, what benefits do you get from the languages you know in writing, speaking, listening . . . for dealing with interculturality as a subject of research and education?

+ Can we really write/speak about interculturality without internalising ourselves in what we claim? Can we place a wall between interculturality as a subject of research and education and interculturality as something we experience in-/directly every minute of our lives in different ways?

We are now moving to the last chapter of the book, unthinking and rethinking, before concluding. We have 'travelled' through five chapters, first observing some of the problems noted in the fragments and then making (provisional) recommendations around adopting a diversity of thoughts of interculturality and criticality of criticality. At this stage, what questions would you want to ask me if you had the opportunity to talk to me? Is there anything that you disagree with? What do you already make of the *paradoxes* of interculturality that I have tried to problematise in my fragments? What are your expectations for the next chapter?

Note

1 A similar review of journal articles and chapters would be useful in the future.

References

Atay, A. (2019). *The discourse of special populations: Critical intercultural communication pedagogy and practice*. New York: Routledge.

Atay, A., & Chen, Y.-W. (Eds.). (2020). *Postcolonial turn and geopolitical uncertainty: Transnational critical intercultural communication pedagogy*. New York: Lexington Books.

Atay, A., & Toyosaki, S. (Eds.). (2020). *Critical intercultural communication pedagogy*. New York: Lexington Books.

Barthes, R. (1977). *Roland Barthes by Roland Barthes*. New York: Farrar, Straus and Giroux.

Barthes, R. (1984). *Le Bruissement de la langue. Essais critiques IV*. Paris: Seuil.

Barthes, R. (2002). *R-B, Roland Barthes*. Paris: Publications du Centre Pompidou.

Dasli, M., & Díaz, A. R. (Eds.). (2016). *The critical turn in language and intercultural communication pedagogy: Theory, research and practice*. London: Routledge.

Dervin, F., & Jacobsson, A. (2021). *Teacher education for critical and reflexive interculturality*. London: Palgrave Macmillan.

Ferri, G. (2018). *Intercultural communication: Critical approaches, future challenges*. London: Palgrave Macmillan.

Fisk, J. (Ed.). (1997). *Composers on music: Eight centuries of writings*. Boston, MA: Northeastern University Press.

Guilherme, M., & Menezes de Souza, L. M. T. (Eds.). (2020). *Glocal languages and critical intercultural awareness: The south answers back*. London: Routledge.

Holmes, P., & Corbett, J. (2022). *Critical intercultural pedagogy for difficult times: Conflict, crisis, and creativity*. London: Routledge.

Holtbrugge, D. (2022). *Intercultural management: Concepts, practice, critical reflection*. London: SAGE.

Lawless, B., & Chen, Y.-W. (2021). *Teaching social justice: Critical tools for the intercultural communication classroom*. New York: Rowman & Littlefield Publishers.

Murdoch, I. (2002). *Henry and Cato*. New York: Vintage Books.

Nakayama, T. K., & Halualani, R. T. (Eds.). (2012). *The handbook of critical intercultural communication*. New York: Wiley-Blackwell.

Piller, I. (2011). *Intercultural communication: A critical introduction*. Edinburgh: Edinburgh University Press.

Sharma, B. K., & Gao, S. (Eds.). (2021). *Language and intercultural communication in tourism: Critical perspectives*. London: Routledge.

Xie, M. (Ed.). (2014). *The agon of interpretations: Towards a critical intercultural hermeneutics*. Toronto: Toronto University Press.

7 Unthink and rethink

In *Poteaux D'Angle* (*Tent Posts*), Henri Michaux (1981, p. 9) writes (translation from French): "Only learn with reservations. An entire life is not enough to unlearn what you naively, submissively, have allowed to be placed in your head – innocent one – without imagining the consequences". It is now time for us to draw conclusions from the previous chapters and to work around two very important processes in dealing with interculturality in research and education: *Unthink* and *rethink*. Although these two verbs are different, we should not look at them separately since they represent two sides of the same coin: There is no unthinking without rethinking and vice versa. *Thinking to and fro* (in all directions, backward, forward, etc.; see Dervin & R'boul, 2023) could be used as a synonym for the two verbs. However, for the sake of clarity, I will keep them (artificially) separate here. Based on the principle of the one-sided surface with no boundaries and the infinite loop of *the Möbius strip* (or 'twisted cylinder'), Figure 7.1 shows what unthinking and rethinking mean in the mirrors of each other (multiple eyes can be seen inside the strip). The prefix *un-*, which indicates reversal, deprivation and removal, is also found in verbs such as unbuckle, unbutton, unchain, undo or unbias and unbind (free from bias and binding). *To unthink interculturality* consists of reversing the way one defines, puts into words, problematises, discusses and analyses the notion *in the mirror of the other* – e.g. a scholar, an educator from another economic-political context. It is about becoming (fully) aware of and recognising the range of (sometimes unstable) ideologies that influence us in the process. Considering critically their consequences on what we say and do, and engage with others (colleagues, students) around interculturality, is vital for *unthinking*. Finally, unthinking is accepting that discomfort and contradictions are part and parcel of intercultural work in research and education. Rethinking goes hand in hand with unthinking by urging us to *think again, anew*. I note, however, that to rethink does not mean to set something in stone for good. In the prefix *re-* in English there is the idea of turning, see twisting.

DOI: 10.4324/9781003371052-9
This chapter has been made available under a CC-BY-NC-ND 4.0 license.

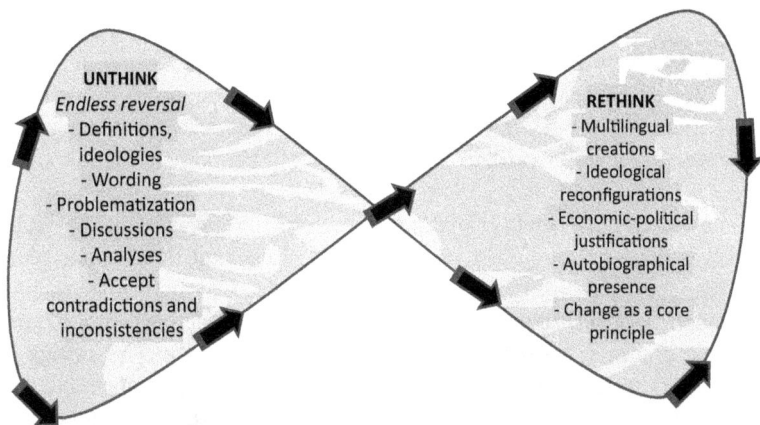

Figure 7.1 The Möbius strip of unthinking and rethinking interculturality

To rethink interculturality consists of trying out new terms from different languages, neologisms, portmanteau words; reconfiguring one's ideological construction of the notion; clarifying the economic-political influences that we support/wish to question; putting oneself in our research and 'acts' of education in more transparent ways and accepting that rethinking must lead us to 'transform' our take on interculturality *ad infinitum* as a core principle.

While you acquaint yourself with this last series of fragments, I suggest you keep Figure 7.1 in mind. What does each fragment tell us about the processes of unthinking and rethinking – especially in the mirror of the other?

~ Fragments VI ~

[Acting]

Staged acts in interculturality.
The verb *to interact* includes the idea of *acting* and *performance*: *To act (between)*. How often are we reminded that interacting is also about *acting*?

If the notion of interculturality could speak, she would tell us many strange and contradictory things that she has heard from those lecturing about and controlling her. *Many secrets*.

Insecurity in the way some white scholars 'give lessons' to scholars from the Global South when they criticise the 'North' – himself included.

We must move beyond mere acquiescence (even critique) to rebellion – *we must refuse!*

[Action]

> Doing interculturality is *cleaving*: Breaking apart and joining together at the same time. Interculturality is both a matter for discussion and for action. Destroying and discarding ideas and concepts does not mean that one is a nihilist. On the contrary, it is a healthy sign of being willing to move forward, to and fro.

Interculturality is both a piano and a violin. While playing the violin involves drawing a bow across the strings or plucking them, piano playing requires 'just' hitting keys from which wooden hammers strike strings. Although both instruments are difficult to play, the actions they require towards a similar mechanism (strings) differ immensely. The strings of interculturality can be plucked, run across and stricken (amongst others). As a subject of research and education, we must try different techniques to 'play' the notion.

Doing research on interculturality corresponds to putting one's head in the lion's mouth.

[Autobiography]

> Writing about and researching interculturality is contributing to one's autobiography. Hiding our *selves* damages the notion. Interculturality is both our self-portrait and a group portrait.

[Becoming]

> How to invent interculturality so she does not run out of steam? *Just let her be.*

Nietzsche's (2007) 'become what you are': *Becoming-being* as one. Interculturality is not a form but *forming*. He wishes for more becoming and unexpected in research on interculturality. *Everything appears too programmed now.*

Like Nietzsche (2007), before he has formulated an idea that contradicts another one that he held about interculturality, he cannot rest. It is the tautology of 'the becoming of interculturality' – one repeats several times that interculturality is about change in this phrase – that keeps him alert in research.

Interculturality is about becoming together, becoming *persons* together with others. But since becoming is part of the human/social being all the time, what differences does interculturality make? One does not become 'intercultural'. One can only be *in-between*.

Inconsistencies and contradictions should not be smoothed over in intercultural research and education. They are part and parcel of the becoming of the notion. *Becoming does not mean moving forward in a straight line.*

Could interculturality be the Chinese 道 (Dao), the 'Way', too? Something that we know we should/could aim for and that we are looking for but can't find.

[Castigating]

> Working on interculturality must be fragile so the work can be 'destroyed' and refashioned. How about we start work on interculturality by castigating research clichés? We need to create fissures in our monochrome ways of thinking. *Renew constantly.*

We need to be 'cunning' in research on interculturality. While today the adjective means sly and deceitful, in Old Norse it used to refer to the act of knowing, being skilful. Knowledge is always cunning in interculturality – *or is interculturality 'sneaky'?*

The shock we should all experience again and again until the day we die: Discovering that the way we (have been made to) think about interculturality is neither the only valid nor the 'best' one.

[Change]

> Interculturality as an open-ended intellectual project needs to keep reinventing herself. No need to find coherence in the mess of interculturality. *Interculturality must be treated ephemerally.*

Change cannot happen in a vacuum; there is always something to be changed. An interesting form of change in Chinese: 变化 (bianhua), which combines sudden change (bian) and subtle change (hua). *Mega-change, multifaceted, various change* of interculturality (Moloney, 2023).

Research on interculturality should not tell people *how to live* and *what to think* but support them in living and thinking *in the plural* – and most importantly: *To change together*. But isn't change happening to us every second of our lives?

Since interculturality is a changing being, one can say that teaching and learning her is somehow always 'otherwise'.

[Classes]

Silent classes of scholarship dominate the unsaid of interculturality.

[Communication]

The beginning of the word *communication* reminds us that it is about *making common, sharing* and *uniting*. Communication is always about two people *a minima* sharing responsibilities for potential mis-/non-understanding.

The uncertainty created by the presence of the other is somewhat smoothed over when we communicate. Communicating (whatever this might mean) fills in the space of uncertainty and might give us a fleeting illusion of 'winning' over the other.

We need research on the influence of scholarly writing and reading on readers, listeners, students, educators and other scholars. Why is it that research on ideologies of interculturality rarely points its gaze at *us*? *How do readers and students experience what we 'throw at' them about interculturality?* is a key question for future research.

[Complex]

The adjective *complex* is from Proto-Indo-European *plek-*, which means *to plait* (itself from Sanskrit for *a turban*). The Greek word *plekein* means *to plait, braid, wind, twine, to interlace*. Can we not like complexity when it is embedded in everything and everyone? *A norm rather than an exception!* The complexity of the world as it is now, as it has always been, makes 'snatching' interculturality impossible.

Nothing is black or white in the way interculturality becomes, but everything is polychrome. *Becomings*. Be open to doubt, non-coincidence with our logical framework, active non-understanding, dreaming.

As much as there are *capitalisms* (Fraser & Jaeggi, 2018; compare the US, China and Finland), there are *interculturalities* around the world.

[Conceptualising]

He has used the verb *to conceptualise* in his earlier work when he has looked at how people discuss interculturality. Maybe this was not a good word if one sees the result of conceptualising in a solid, one-directional sense ... *conceptual* is from Latin *conceptus*, a collecting, gathering, conceiving, *concipere*, to take in and *conceiven*, take (seed) into the womb, become pregnant. *Take into the mind, form a correct notion of* is from the mid-14th century, that of *form as a general notion in the mind* is from the late 14th century. Conceptualising is not a straight line. Conceptualising should include showing the complex paths on the way to discourses of *interculturality as change*, the contradictions we face, the revisions, the shifting we experience. When we conceptualise, we recreate *again and again. We do not set in stone*. Conceptualising is collecting ideas and thoughts. *There is no end to it. Unthink <> Rethink.*

When he discusses how someone conceptualises interculturality, he must 'dig' into the input of others in this complex process. How much have they influenced him? One never conceptualises alone.

Comparing the etymologies of the words *concept* and *notion*, he notes that *concept* is from Latin *concipere* for *to take in and hold*; *become pregnant* and *notion* was coined in Latin by Cicero as a loan-translation of Greek *ennoia* for act of thinking, notion, conception. He prefers to speak of the notion of interculturality, as something to think *with* rather than as a concept that 'encloses'.

[Connotations]

It is the connotations of the words that we use that dictate interculturality rather than their meanings.

Morandi colours (a muted and pale colour palette, a layer of grey tones from the Italian artist Giorgio Morandi, 1890–1964) are not fixed colours but are based on *colour relationship*. They have rich, peaceful connotations. If he could paint interculturality in research, he would use these subtle colours that do not jump in our face, that do not show off, that are in a relationship, *an in-betweenness*.

[Contradictions]

Polarities coexisting. Interculturality is about accommodating tensions and contradictions. Interculturality requires thinking through uncertainty and contradictions.

Why is the fact that we are full of contradictions never included in intercultural research/theory? Why do we want to make her coherent and straightforward? We are always in between opposite states. We must accept contradictions and live with them.

One week he tells a friend that he wants to stay in country X, that he is so happy to be there. He meets the same friend a week later and tells him that he would love to go to country Y because he feels so cheerful there. The friend reminds him of what he claimed the week before. He tells his friend that he remembers very well. *He is just a human being; he contradicts himself; he changes.*

Love and hostility go hand in hand; they are not separated. They do not happen in a straight line.

That people contradict themselves in the way they discuss interculturality is a norm. We all do. We must feel vulnerable in interculturality. Every one of us has a dark side. We all have 'bad' thoughts that we never voice. We all perform in front of others. We say we like them while, in fact, we have issues being with them. *No one is perfect*. We are all torn apart between 'good' and 'bad' (whatever these might mean). *We are bad and ignorant. Not just the other!* "I love upright, clever and independent humans", says a friend about someone she admires. He replies: "She is also probably dishonest, silly and needy".

You can't be fully essentialist or non-essentialist since, as a human being, you are full of contradictions, which makes you both essentialist and non-essentialist. *Juggle with the ordered and the chanced, the factual and the suggestive.*

Othering is a necessary and yet painful crash course.

The feeling of schizophrenia that he feels when he hears students rehearsing on the one hand the litanies of American/'Western' ideologies of intercultural communication education and on the other sharing completely different (and more diverse) discourses about their own experiences of interculturality (see Dervin & Tan, 2023).

[Curiosity]

> We should feed in new knowledge about interculturality by making proposals, rejecting them, returning to them, making counterproposals, creating ruptures, divergences, disagreements, agreements, *ad infinitum*.

A Chinese idea: 厚积薄发 (hòujī-bófā), *build up fully and release sparingly*. Good advice for all interculturalists. Accumulate knowledge from any place in the world to lay a sound foundation and *then* make new accomplishments, beyond the taken-for-granted, the rehearsed, the 'too obvious' – release! *Confront (your) knowledge with (your) knowledge* ad infinitum.

Learn to watch with curiosity and/or embrace the way we behave/think/speak.

Find yourself in what you read, in the data you analyse. You are always there. The absent-present.

[Destiny]

In Chinese the word for *fate, destiny* is: 缘分. 缘 means *edge* or *reason* and 分 *divide, share*. It is about experiencing many coincidences together. 'Fate' is also an inevitable connection. A meeting of two people for which both have the responsibility to fulfil a promise of togetherness. *A beautiful (idealistic) definition for interculturality.*

Interculturality will always be cleverer than us scholars. We'll never beat her.

[Dream]

> Interculturality as a dream, a fantasy. I dream of a better us together in research and education.

We need some kind of prose for interculturality in research. As much as interculturality is floating, our thoughts and writing should hang, glide and drift.

A book should offer a catalogue of unsolved problems. Why should we always pretend to know how to *solve*? *Dreams of interculturality needed.*

[Drills]

Interculturality is not about performing tedious drills: He sees a picture of some Chinese scholars on Zoom pulling their faces with their hands to mimic a smile. He asks a Chinese friend what this could mean – *if this is a Chinese 'thing'?* He believes that it is a non-verbal sign used in China (like the finger heart made with the thumb and the index finger to show love). According to his friend, it is not, *they are just trying to create a sense of togetherness in Zoom by inventing a common sign.*

It is not enough to change the instruments and a few other tricks when we work on interculturality; we need to change e.g. the tradition of how e.g. things sound, how the sounds are organised, etc. We must watch how we speak about interculturality. We need 'detergent discourses' (Barthes, 1977,

p. 122) to get rid of our biases and impressions in research and education, and apply it *again and again*.

[Eruption]

> Interculturality should be an eruption. It should awaken echoes within us: *Who are we with the other? How similar/different could we be with the other? How can we dare to disagree so we can move forward together?* Interculturality is constructive, spontaneous, tenacious and innovative.

Do we really need a book about interculturality which has a beginning and an end? As if there was a clear problem to confront and a solution to propose? How about we don't have anything to offer? How about we experience endless eruptions?

[Escape]

> How can we escape from what (we think) we know? We must self-teach interculturality to do away with models, to be as authentic as we can and to take responsibility for one's views. *You* (有) in Chinese refers to an unattached, relaxed and unencumbered approach to people and things ('to keep at arm's length' in English). *The right approach to our 'scientific' takes on interculturality*. Let's not get too attached; let other systems of thought enter our mind while keeping our distance.

[Ethics]

> The only real ethical question for interculturality is: *Should we give 'orders' about her?*

Criticality does not mean *non-Westernality*. Criticality can be a form of camouflage for 'neo-Westernality' in intercultural research. *Criticality as protection against one's own critiques.*

Move away from treating research participants as passive agents to the active co-constructors they are.

[Etymology]

> Navigating between the intimate relations of words in a dictionary, by exploring their etymology, could help us unthink and rethink interculturality. How words evolve, change and relate has very much to do with the notion.

[Experience]

Bergson (1985, p. 36) mentions an anonymous philosopher who responded to critiques of his work by arguing that his ideas were *contra to* people's experience: *"their experience is wrong"*. This is what many research participants would be told by us researchers if confronted with their experiences of interculturality. *However, their experience is* right.

Interculturality can only make sense if we relate her to our own experience. Looking at her from above does not make much sense. Working on interculturality should not be detached from our realities, our own experience of the world, and self and other.

His life and work must intersect when he works on interculturality.

[Explore]

The need to explore and experiment everyday – *never stop!*

[Far-but-close]

Someone asks him if he speaks French. He replies that he doesn't use the language. He reads and listens to it every day, but he never speaks it. His interlocutor replies: "oh what a shame! You must miss it". *No, he doesn't miss speaking a language.* Actually, he is happy he doesn't have to 'speak' it. Today, he feels that reading and listening to French give him more freedom to explore, hesitate, contradict himself, reflect endlessly and silently, without the 'live' interruption of the other. Of course, that other is always there, but in a remote position, *far-but-close to him*. Reading and listening to French, he can decide when to take his distance, when to pause, when to be more honest. It is a privileged position in a language. He cherishes this position. Other languages that he uses for speaking on a daily basis, which make him 'closer' to the other, put more (needed) restrictions on his thinking. These 'speaking' sessions obviously feed in his reading and listening to French too.

[Flute]

Why is the flute always *enchanted* or *magic* but not the guitar? He dreams of a magic accordion or a magic Guqin (古琴) as much as he fantasises over sounds of interculturality played on different instruments (languages, ideologies, etc.).

[Fresh]

A colleague tells him that a research plan that they had both reviewed is 'fresh' compared to others she had read. He found it 'stale' and reminds her that "one can suffocate from freshness too".

[Good/bad]

When he works on his art, he knows what is good and what is bad in his production. In rare instances, something 'not good' turns out to be 'good' when he reworks it entirely. Interestingly his friends always like the pieces that he finds uninteresting. *Interculturality*.

No one is good, no one is bad; everybody is good, everybody is bad.

[Infidelity]

We should be unfaithful to our own ideas. Interculturality should not be a straight line or an ideological cocoon.

[Intermezzo]

Interculturality is an *enantiomer*: She presents non-superimposable mirror images (e.g. the right and left hand) of self-other, which cannot be reoriented to appear identical. Interculturality is an illusion of identicality of which we must beware.

Interculturality should just be an intermezzo, i.e. moments in between, nothing before, nothing after. *Interculturality must put us in a position of equilibrium.*

[(The) invisible chain]

We are all interdependent, interpenetrated. *Even with our worst enemy.* A person his age in e.g. Kathmandu relates to him. They have never met – and probably never will – but they share the same humanity, the same earth, the same problems. They both impact the environment, others, things, living species. They are part of the same invisible chains of interculturality.

[Landscapes]

He still doesn't know how to appreciate landscape painting. He prefers portraits. However, in his mind he misses landscapes and places –

not people. He often daydreams of the most meaningful places in his life (Beijing, Hong Kong, London, Paris, Rauma, Vääksy, Venice . . .). He wants the freedom to reimagine his engagement with these places.

[Language]

He has a love and hate relationship with words in English – the language he uses the most for writing these days. He doesn't trust them, he fears them, while he worships some of them momentarily. Yet, the archaeology of words in English and their polysemy bring many 'wow' moments and excitement in him. *From the illusion of uniformity to interculturality.*

We must invent new words, new terms to talk about interculturality. We cannot just retain and recycle the same words – or repackage them. Working on interculturality relies on both the archaeological and predicting the future. Neologisms needed, e.g. combining two already existing words, creating semantic neologisms, borrowing from other languages.

Language *depaysement* is central to research and education related to interculturality. Words do not 'flavour' the same between languages – in fact: *even within just one*. To become aware of this important aspect, etymology reminds us of the inherent instability of words: *Ill* used to mean *evil*, now *sick*; *dogma* used to refer to *a philosophical tenet*, now to *a belief many refuse to question*. There is interculturality within every word.

If he sees 'must' and 'should' in discourses of interculturality, he now runs away. 'Could' and 'may/might' – he would like to see more. *Sometimes he has to escape from his own writing.*

We need to listen to the 'infra-language' of people, to their 'banal' and 'meaningless' (to use scholars' discourses!) language rather than our own, instead of moulding their voices with ours and 'violating' their voices when we speak of interculturality (Latour, 2005, p. 30).

Relearn to speak to avoid the flow of Westernisms and Americanisms concerning interculturality. Learn new languages (even *within* one single language) to speak about her!

Translating again and again tells us *again and again* that the reality is rich and unstable.

On a daily basis, even in just one language, we speak different forms of a given language, with different people, in different contexts. It is not surprising then that there is so much instability and polysemy when we speak about interculturality. *The unpretentious way of things.*

The question of giving access to different kinds of knowledge might not really be the core problem of interculturality. One can have (the illusion) of having that access. Access to dominating knowledge (ideologies?) about interculturality is easy in any case since the market is flooded with publications and talks from dominating voices (see Peng et al.'s 2020 article about who 'rules' the sub-field of intercultural competence). However, what matters, he believes, is 1. What to do with this multifaceted knowledge? 2. How to make it enter into meaningful dialogues with other kinds of knowledge that can lead to new forms of knowledge? 3. How to empower people who are not part of more global discussions around interculturality to voice their dis-agreements and add to the discussions? Another issue concerns being trained to identify the potential political and ideological manipulations hidden behind knowledge (for example, when it emerges from the OECD, the Council of Europe or any (supranational) institution). The central issue is (again) language: *What meanings and connotations of concepts/notions, ideas, arguments, etc.? How to re-enunciate from a translingual/multilingual perspective while being aware of politics-ideologies?*

We must accept the impossibility of talking about interculturality. *Language does not allow us to do so*. A 'critical' scholar is still limited by their use of a given language and the ideas that are ingrained in their mind. The interest is not so much in learning different languages but in learning to reflect on the different meanings and connotations of e.g. words as used in other languages. The doxa might think that the more languages we know the better, but sometimes, knowing just one language while being able to 'evaluate' the connotations of a given word in different languages is better than 'knowing' *20 different languages. We might speak languages without caring about language.*

Language is always violent. When we take the floor, we use words and sentences that create potential threats in the other – as much as their words might have the same effects on us. Power relations are established through language. By failing to reflect on and dissect our use of language when we speak about interculturality, we contribute to create even wider gaps between us.

Do not banish the inherent complexity and instability of language from your work!

[Masks]

Face and *fake* share the same etymology: Latin *facere*, to make.

Why do we complain about having to wear a COVID mask when we always wear a mask with others anyway?

With the 2020 pandemic and us wearing COVID masks, he believes that we have learnt to smile with our eyes.

Today he was interviewing a student who was wearing a COVID mask. He sees half her face; he imagines her face. He never really pays attention to eyes. Suddenly she removes the mask! He sees a completely different person. *NOT the person he had imagined through her eyes.* It disturbs him at first: he feels that he has been talking to two different people. *Accept plurality! Accept masks! We must imagine a plurality of faces for the other and for ourselves.*

Researchers do have a self (selves?) and need to both recognise and accept it.

[Matrix]

Is there a need for a theoretical matrix for such a changing and unstable subject as interculturality? How can we write about interculturality when interculturality is itself an impossibility? We will never reach fully the *inter-* of the notion.

[Mouth]

One can have different 'mouth experiences' with food: *Chewable, soft, crispy* . . . Interculturality should also rely on different *flavours* and *mouth actions.*

[Moving forward]

We have a responsibility to shake things as far as interculturality is concerned. We must move it forward, without following a concrete direction. *Explore, dig, unthink, rethink.* If we are too comfortable with our thinking, we cannot move forward. *Discomfort! Uneasiness!*

In the Russian word for *painting*, Живопись (zivopis), one finds the idea of 'writing of the living' – a principle we should adopt for research on interculturality, beyond the current image of 'interculturality-as-a-zombie' often found in some literature.

For an approach to interculturality that is weaving itself ceaselessly!

Whatever centre of interculturality we create, the earth will continue rotating, disregarding these centres and letting interculturality happen.

[Naming]

Does naming something intercultural make it *intercultural*? Do we need to name something as 'intercultural' for it to be *intercultural*? Can the unlabelled be intercultural too?

[Need]

A friend from Ethiopia tells me how people will ask him "which clan are you from"? when they meet in his country. *This human need to classify* . . .

The real issue is not what interculturality is, but why do we need such a notion today?

[Neologism]

A student uses the interesting neologism of *interculturating*. Intercultural as a verb, as action, as movement, as something that does not stop. *I interculturate, you interculturate, we interculturate.*

[piānfēng]

Interculturality urges us to adopt 偏锋 (piānfēng) – a term in Chinese calligraphy for a brush stroke to the side. Piānfēng suggests thinking laterally, creatively, not to follow a ready-made way of thinking.

[Portmanteau]

A word that results from blending two or more words, or parts of words. A portmanteau word expresses some combination of the meanings of its parts. Examples in English include *chortle* (from chuckle and snort), *smog* (from smoke and fog), *brunch* (from breakfast and lunch), *mockumentary* (from mock and documentary), and *spork* (from spoon and fork). We need portmanteau words to work on interculturality – the notion urges us to mix, to create, to open up. Some that he has invented: *Critizenship (critical use of citizenship, beyond the statement of the need for 'active citizenship'), culturitics (the enmeshment of culture and politics), differilitude (difference and similitude as companions), homoginary (a homogeneous imaginary)* . . .

[Questions]

Ask questions, but don't always expect answers. Do we need answers to questions? Can we get answers to our questions? *Not always. We need to be inspired to push forward.*

Why do we use a given perspective? Why do we refer to a 'pet' researcher? Why *them* and not something or someone else?

[Random]

Audacity needed! Randomness is required in the way we explore interculturality. There should be a certain randomness in the way one finds ideas for interculturality in research and education: *A piece of art, something someone said to us on the streets, a face, an angry voice . . .*

Read all books on intercultural communication education first and then liberate yourselves from the few 'doxic' perspectives that you might have come across by reading *elsewhere, randomly . . .*
There are other worlds in his fragments, in these bits and pieces. They are like the infinite virtuality of interculturality.
No need to try to imitate interculturality. Just let her guide us.

[Real]

A Chinese friend had his birthday a few days ago – at least that's what he thought. He had an idea of when it was precisely, but he could not be sure since the friend relies on the lunar calendar to determine his birthday every year – *the date is never identical as the calendar changes yearly.* The friend told him that his birthday was on a Wednesday. He asked: "your real birthday?". The friend acquiesced. What does *real* mean to the both of them here? To him 'real' meant the date on his passport, *the 'Western' date*. But he realised later that to his friend his 'real' birthday was the Lunar calendar one that changes. *Abolish the 'real'! My 'real' is not necessarily your 'real'.*

[Reflexes]

Let's leave our conceptual reflexes aside – our favourite concepts, notions, theories, 'gurus'! *Towards the end of karaokeing songs about interculturality.*

Feelings must be taken into account in theories. There is no theory without feelings.

[Refrain]

We have the right not to like or feel comfortable with certain people. If we have the power to refrain from engaging with them, we have the right to do so. Unfortunately, few of us are privileged in the sense that we can limit our engagement with people we don't feel we should spend time with. *Others suffer in silence.*

[Saw teeth]

Doing interculturality must be like going up and down the teeth of a never-ending saw.

[Self-satisfaction]

Interculturality should never lead to self-satisfaction – as in: *We are done!* No, we are NOT done with her. We can never be satisfied with 'our' views on interculturality, considering the state of the world. *We must fight on.*

[Sensuality]

We need more feelings and emotions in intercultural research. *Eroticisation* of the notion, as Barthes (1977) would put it.

In Chinese the word *intelligence* consists of the two characters for *to hear* and *to see*. Maybe this is what those who talk about *intercultural intelligence* mean?

Listen to art, don't just look at it! Don't just listen to music, look at it, taste it in your mouth! Interculturality should also make use of all senses.

Libido spectandi: The illusion that it is only when seeing that we experience the 'reality' of things. After two years online, he is happy just to see and/or listen to others through a computer. He is not convinced that seeing *live* or *face-to-face* adds to interculturality, especially if we do not listen to each other and aren't ready to change . . . Physical co-presence can be an illusion of interculturality.

We need new *dramatis personae* in research on interculturality (a new list of characters in the play).

[Silence]

Learn to be silent and to enjoy stillness.

Repeating what people say in research data is tedious and uninteresting. He would rather we identified what they do not say at the surface of their discourses.

[Stare]

We must gaze and stare into interculturality, not just peep at it.

In interculturality research, let's listen – rather than *just* hear; let's stare – rather than *just* see. Both hearing and seeing appear to be too passive to deal with the complexities of the notion.

[Step outside]

We need to step outside our comfort zones, our pet concepts, theories and scholars – which may be 'pet' because we are unaware of alternatives.

Ways of dealing with interculturality beyond the 'West' should not be treated as metonymies – as in: *'A' Global South perspective on interculturality. It is never 'a' perspective but perspectives*. Step outside *within* the Global South too.

Our mind must be available, leave some space for other ways of thinking; we cannot bury ourselves in just one way of thinking about interculturality.

[Stillness]

For Marina Abramovic (2018, p. 45): "In stillness everything becomes so visible and important". The multiple lockdowns that he has experienced since 2020 have definitely opened up his eyes *interculturally speaking* – in stillness with himself, his memories of others and others on his phone and computer.

[(The) 'tap']

There is so much that we don't say to each other. So much that we keep silent. At times, we find a 'tap' to turn on (another person), through which we can evacuate what we don't tell others.

[Think]

It is not about defining interculturality *precisely*, enclosing her in a static definition but about getting into the habit of unthinking and rethinking her. By pressuring people to produce 'results', we are pushed not to think further. *However, we must think against ourselves. We must think against language. We must think against 'results'.*

Don't tell us what and how to think, just let us think!

To think otherwise is not necessarily to oppose.
Think in all directions!

[Together]

Interculturality is what we can and might become *together*.

[Towards the inside]

He doesn't want to talk about interculturality anymore, especially if it is to 'brainwash' others. He wants to speak *from the sides*, not *towards the inside*. *Unwash* our brains.

[Underground]

Sometimes interculturality is so obvious that we forget that she is there. In such moments interculturality does her work 'underground'. *When we are oblivious of interculturality, interculturality wins!*

[Vocabulary]

Don't look down on other scholars or educators for using certain words and phrases to talk about interculturality. Don't lecture them about what they should use or not use. Listen to them, ask questions, try to negotiate meanings and connotations and, more importantly, to understand their starting points.

When we translate a term, why do we often end up with just *one equivalent*? Why can't we retain several words? Do we always need to choose the 'right' word – which often ends up being an 'ideologically-correct' term?

A tongue is never 'mother'. Writing to, speaking with/for others, you always need to tame a language. The idea of the mother tongue gives the illusion of simplicity and naturalness. What a tongue is could be sempiternal arguments between a mum and a dad (or mum(s) and mum(s), dad(s) and dad(s) and other figures), before and between moments of happiness. 'Mother tongue' is not just a word but also an ideology.

The omnipresence of the English word 'happy' in China makes him wonder [the latest he noticed was 'Learning Chinese is happy']: If people are happy, why (re-)claim it all the time – and in another language?

We have to use our own terminology, our own vocabulary to talk about diversity/interculturality not to overshadow realities with other ideological filters.

Our research on interculturality needs to be 'inhabited' by our own conceptions of the notion. In French, *être habité par* (word-for-word: 'to be inhabited by') refers to the fact that something lives inside of us. This could help us take a distance from ideologies that we feel we have to ingurgitate.

He comes across the discourse instruments *femvertising* and *Transfronterixz*. He is confused. He tries to find out what they mean but no one seems to explain them in the literature. As if they were obvious, *taken for granted*. Door closed to *interculturalities*.

"I will collect data in culturally diverse schools" (another word for 'migrants' here). Aren't all schools *culturally diverse*?

We say 'racist' but we don't refer to 'race' in many parts of Europe. How about 'ethnicist' since we only talk about 'ethnicity'?

Interculturality is an *amphibogy* (something that can be understood in multiple ways): We all hear the same word but we hear something else.

How often do we think about what hides behind the words that we use? For example, *to denigrate* contains the idea of "blacken, make black"; *a functionary* an official "function".

[Slow down]

> *Let's slow down together and put all the cards on the table.*
> *Where do we stand with interculturality? What are we doing with her?*
> *Can we talk to each other about her?*
> *Interculturality must be considered with lento.*
> *Slow down!*

~ Interthinking ~

For this last interthinking session, I suggest you start by going back to Figure 7.1. Summarise what you take away for both unthinking and rethinking from the fragments. Try to think of 'concrete' suggestions that were made.

The following excerpts were collected from the fragments to summarise what I consider to be some of the most important aspects of unthinking and rethinking. For each excerpt, review for yourselves what they mean and entail for your work as a researcher, teacher and/or student of interculturality:

> "Doing research on interculturality corresponds to putting one's head in the lion's mouth".
>
> "The real issue is not what interculturality is but why do we need such a notion today?".
>
> "One does not become 'intercultural'. One can only be *in-between*".

"He prefers to speak of the notion of interculturality as something to think *with* rather than as a concept that 'encloses'".

"Working on interculturality must be fragile".

"We should be unfaithful to our own ideas".

"When we conceptualise, we recreate *again and again. We do not set in stone*".

"Confront (your) knowledge with (your) knowledge *ad infinitum*".

"Let's not get too attached; let other systems of thoughts enter our mind".

"We must move beyond mere acquiescence (even critique) towards rebellion – *we must refuse!*".

"Writing about and researching interculturality is contributing to one's autobiography".

Now take some time to explore the following questions:

+ Having navigated through the pages of this book, have you come across anything that made you even more aware of the fact that *the way we (have been made to) think about interculturality is neither the only valid one nor the 'best' one*? How often have you had the opportunity to note this very same argument in other research pieces or in what someone was saying? Can you remember precise examples?
+ In the chapter I suggest that the issue of how readers and students experience what scholars 'throw at' them about interculturality should be researched further. Could you reflect on your own experience of reading or listening to someone talking about interculturality? How did they make you feel? Were you convinced by their line of argumentation/demonstration? Why (not)? What would you have liked to discuss with them?
+ Spend some minutes exploring the archaeology, etymology, and multifaceted use of these concepts (which are often used in research on interculturality) in English and other languages. Can this teach you anything new and different about them?

- Citizenship
- Community
- Conflict
- Culture
- Diversity
- Ethnicity
- Harmony
- Identity
- Tolerance

+ What 'trigger warnings' would you recommend we could adopt to avoid 'ideological cocooning' in our work on interculturality, i.e. remaining within the safe space of the 'orders' we have been fed concerning interculturality? In other words, how to listen to oneself carefully and 'revise' our potentially one-sided views on the notion?
+ Would you want to 'invent' new terms for talking about interculturality in English and other languages? Which ones and why?
+ How comfortable are you with the argument that we don't need to find or provide answers to the questions we ask or to others' questions when it comes to interculturality as a subject of research and education? Do you find this type of uncertainty to be 'nerve-racking'?
+ Go back to the last piece that you have written about interculturality (an article, a book, an essay) and consider these questions: *Why do we use a given perspective? Why do we use a pet researcher? Why* them *and not something or someone else?*

I chose to include the fragment on 'slowing down with interculturality' at the very end of this chapter as an important signal to my readers and I do hope that, by pulling you in 'all directions', my book has made you realise that it is important to not rush into conclusions about or delimitations of the notion. What concrete actions could we take to systematise 'slowing down' in research and education on interculturality to allow unthinking and rethinking to mature? What would you suggest?

References

Abramovic, M. (2018). *Marina Abramovic: Writings 1960–2014.* Köln: Walther König.
Barthes, R. (1977). *Roland Barthes by Roland Barthes.* New York: Farrar, Straus and Giroux.
Bergson, H. (1985). *Le rire.* Paris: PUF. (Original work published 1900)
Dervin, F., & R'boul, H. (2023). *Through the looking-glass of interculturality: Autocritiques.* Singapore: Springer.
Dervin, F., & Tan, H. (2023). *Supercriticality and interculturality.* Singapore: Springer.
Fraser, N., & Jaeggi, R. (2018). *Capitalism: A conversation in critical theory.* Cambridge: Polity.
Latour, B. (2005). *Reassembling the social: An introduction to actor-network-theory.* Oxford: Oxford University Press.
Michaux, H. (1981). *Poteaux d'Angle.* Paris: Gallimard.
Moloney, R. (2023). Teaching interculturality: Changes in perspective (A story of change). In: F. Dervin, M. Yuan, & Sude (Eds.), *Teaching interculturality 'otherwise'.* London: Routledge.

Nietzsche, F. (2007). *Ecce Homo*. Oxford: Oxford University Press.
Peng, R.-Z., Zhu, C., & Wu, W.-P. (2020). Visualizing the knowledge domain of intercultural competence research: A bibliometric analysis. *International Journal of Intercultural Relations, 74*, 58–68.

8 Conclusion

Towards an approach to interculturality that is weaving itself ceaselessly

In one of the chapters of this book, a fragment said: "A book should offer a catalogue of unsolved problems". What did you expect from this book? Why did you reach out to this book? What did the title *say* to you before you read it? *The paradoxes of interculturality*. For Virginia Woolf (2021, p. 9):

> Few people ask from books what books can give us. Most commonly we come to books with blurred and divided minds, asking of fiction that it shall be true, of poetry that it shall be false, of biography that it shall be flattering, of history that it shall enforce our own prejudices. If we could banish all such preconceptions when we read, that would be an admirable beginning.

How do your expectations of what my book would do to you match the reality? Did I answer (in-/directly) some of the questions that you had in mind or am I leaving you with even more questions? Did the book make you change your mind about a particular aspect of interculturality or did it convince you that you are/were 'right'?

Let me start by trying to form an incomplete picture of the points made about the 'character' that interested us in this book. Considering the complexities of the fragments and the constant back-and-forth movements that they represent, I do not consider what follows as a summary as such but as a way of pinpointing issues that have *returned* in the book – spiral-like – and that need addressing for unthinking and rethinking interculturality.

The definition of interculturality does not have to be the starting point of research and education. No one will be right, no one will be wrong about what she is. Instead, speculating as to why we need her represents an interesting first entry point. At the same time, we can ask the same question about companion terms such as *multicultural, transcultural* and *cross-cultural*. In most chapters, we noticed that interculturality is never 'obvious' and that 'doctrines' that have attempted to 'cage' her into e.g. models can turn out to be counterproductive and working against interculturality herself. The doxa around the notion – to which I have contributed and still contribute in this book – is strong and deserves to be identified, analysed and described, bearing in mind with Woolf (1967, p. 286) that "it is far harder to kill a phantom than a reality". This is why we must dialogue around the notion again and again, confronting our 'doxic' ideas about her, accepting disagreements, contradictions and inconsistencies, experiencing some degree of discomfort in the process and being 'unfaithful' to our ideologies as much as we can. I have suggested that it might be better to use the notion of interculturality as something to think *with* rather than as a concept that 'encloses' the world, others and ourselves. Interculturality must be used as an *either AND or* notion in research and education rather than an inflexible tool. Since the notion is always embedded in specific economic-political contexts, any statement on interculturality is ideological – a list of behavioural, attitudinal and discursive orders. An awareness of this inherent characteristic of the notion is a must for anyone involved in research and education. Many fragments reviewed aspects of so-called ('Western') critical perspectives, showing that they often end up biting their own tails; becoming dominating ideologies and protecting already privileged discursive and symbolic positions in the global fields attached to interculturality (e.g. today's non-essentialism). 'Competitive' ideologies from outside the 'Western' province – although many ideologies of interculturality from within are also silenced – are many and yet they rarely find their ways into the spotlight. I have thus argued in the fragments that those of us who are privileged enough to be 'heard' need to be silent for a while and leave the floor to other unnoticed voices, especially from the Global South. *We must express our gratitude for every unknown 'piece' of knowledge about interculturality that we are given access to.*

Applying the principles of the *inter-* and *-ality* of interculturality to this process of knowledge production was suggested. As soon as a ritornello of interculturality starts dominating (e.g. *intercultural competence, democracy* and soon *decolonial*), it needs to be challenged, transformed, re-negotiated, discarded since it could never be in tune with the polysemous and multi-faceted ritornellos from the rest of the world. There are so many *stories of interculturality* to be discovered around the world that we will be kept busy for decades to come! Infusing diversities of thought beyond competition and in the spirit of change is also an interesting direction to consider. We cannot just be passive spectators to the epistemic injustice of one corner of the world determining what interculturality is about. This entails confronting our criticality with criticality, detaching ourselves from specific glocal-economic-political anchors, creating again and again, playing with and interrogating the way we speak about interculturality, reminding ourselves that we are also, each and every one of us, part of the mysterious character of interculturality

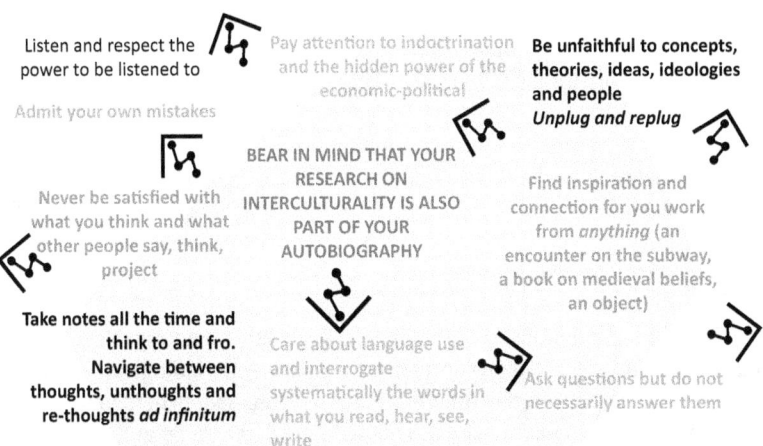

Figure 8.1 Interculturality weaving itself ceaselessly

and that our research and teaching *always involve getting involved with her*. We must liberate others – *and in the process ourselves!* I finished the last chapter by reminding us that the complex processes of letting diversities flourish, criticality of criticality and unthinking-rethinking deserve to occur in slow paces. We must be adventurous, take the time to read (beyond our field(s)), experience through e.g. art, engage in (heated) conversations, look at oneself in the mirror. More importantly maybe, we should accept that as an unstable and hyper-complex notion, interculturality reminds us, following Kierkegaard (1939, p. 194): "It is the duty of the human understanding to understand that there are things which it cannot understand . . ."

Figure 8.1 leaves the reader with a few takeaways from the discussions in the book. I have labelled these elements 'an approach to interculturality that is weaving itself ceaselessly' and offer it as a (temporary and unfinished) description of some components of proposed 'toolbox for out-of-the-box ideas'.

This book was written as a 'toolbox for out-of-the-box ideas', based on fragments about interculturality as a subject of research and education. For most readers, I assume that both the structure of the book and its style would have been unfamiliar – although one could maintain that things like Twitter and other social media 'tools' in different parts of the world adopt a similar writing format. Many thinkers, intellectuals and scholars have also used this genre for constructing their thoughts in less predictable and (perhaps) more complex ways (e.g. Cioran, 2018). Using fragments, I have felt freer in my writing, and somehow closer to you, my readers. By allowing me to work 'spiral-like' (instead of in some kind of [falsely] straightforward path), I feel that I was able to share my uncertainties, hesitations as well as some (auto-)critiques about interculturality – sharpening them (temporarily) in the process. For Borges (1964, p. 214):

> A book is more than a verbal structure or series of verbal structures; it is the dialogue it establishes with its reader and the intonation it imposes upon his voice and the changing and durable images it leaves in his memory. A book is not an isolated being: it is a relationship, an axis of innumerable relationships.

This kind of relationship between you the readers and myself is beneficial when working on such a polysemic, unstable and ideologically-oriented notion. I do hope that the 'interthinking' sections from the chapters have also added to 'our' relationships. The dialogue between an author and their readers is also a form of interculturality that we need to address in research and education.

You will be left alone in a few moments, outside the dis-/comfort of this book. Some of you might return to it (read some fragments again); others might just put it on their bookshelves and never look at it again. But now, in a sense, the book is *yours and mine – ours*. You own its content as much as I do. You can criticise it, judge it, discuss it with others. At the same time, you can do whatever you want with the main character of the book: interculturality. In the introduction we started with Beckett's play *Waiting for Godot* – this absent-present (imaginary) individual for whom the main characters are waiting. Although they never seem to be able to meet him, they come back every day to the same meeting spot, waiting for him. I suggested in the introduction that I could have called this book *Waiting for Interculturality* because I feel that we have been involved in the same processes as Estragon and Vladimir in Beckett's play. Interculturality has been in our mouth and mind in the previous pages, but she never really appeared personally. Adapting Beckett's (1996, p. 136) message to a French journalist about *Waiting for Godot* quoted in the introduction, I write:

> [Add names of the characters, concepts, doxic elements . . . encountered in the fragments], their time and their space I was able to get to know them a little only at a great distance from the need to understand. You may feel they owe you explanations. Let them manage it. Without me. They and I are through with each other.

They are now all yours. But I am not through with interculturality yet.

References

Beckett, S. (1996, June 24 and July 1). To Michel Polac (1952). *The New Yorker*, p. 136.
Borges, J. L. (1964). *Labyrinths: Selected stories and other writings*. New York: New Directions.
Cioran, E. (2018). *A short story of decay*. London: Penguin Classics.
Kierkegaard, S. (1939). *The journals of Kierkegaard*. Oxford: Oxford University Press.
Woolf, V. (1967). *Collected essays (Volume II)*. London: The Hogarth Press.
Woolf, V. (2021). *How should one read a book?* London: Renard Press.

Appendix
List of terms proposed by the author

Alienly: Adverb used to urge interculturalists to step back from their 'usual' ways of looking at and analysing interculturality, playing the stranger with the notion.

Amphibogy: From Greek for *irregular speech* but also *hitting at both ends* (ambiguous). In the book it is used to refer to the fact that interculturality often leads to contradictions and inconsistences (*this* and/or *that*) – in un-/intended ways. Accepting the amphibogy of interculturality is the *sine qua non* of research and education.

Anamorphosis: In Art, a perspective that gives a distorted image of the subject in a painting, where they might be reflected in a curved mirror. Our access to interculturality being limited since it is inaccessible as a 'full' entity, anamorphosis in the way we e.g. describe her is a common phenomenon.

Anchors: Refers to preferred, 'pet' theories, researchers, ideologies, in intercultural research. Like anchors, these hold us in a particular geo-economic-political place and prevent us from exploring other areas, and from *looking around aimlessly*.

Atelophilia: The appreciation of imperfection. Not being afraid of making mistakes or not being able to find answers to all the questions one faces when one works on interculturality as a subject of research and education. From Greek for *the end, fulfilment* and *imperfect, incomplete* (without an end).

Cleaving: To break apart and join together at the same time. A somewhat contradictory process common in intercultural encounters.

Conceptual reflexes: Habit of using concepts related to interculturality automatically ('robot-like') without questioning their meaning, connotation, inclusion and 'real' use in our work. The concepts become automatons that remove some of the fluidity of interculturality.

Criticality of criticality: Showing and 'doing' criticality of one's own criticality or of others' criticality that we favour. Goes hand in hand with

Appendix: List of terms proposed by the author 127

reflexivity. A critical thought about interculturality should always be inspected through another layer of criticality.
Criticentrism: Placing one's own critique at the centre. Believing or making others believe that it is infallible and can be adopted in/adapted to any context of study in relation to interculturality.
Detokenising: A 'token' is an individual from a symbolically underprivileged background in research on interculturality (e.g. the Global South) who is used to promote a privileged ('White', 'Western') ideological agenda. By their own presence, the 'token' contributes to show that the 'privileged' care for e.g. epistemic diversity and wish for change, while in reality, they might long for a *status quo* and resist antagonism. Detokenising is the ethical decision to not include and/or use the 'token' for promoting one's ideas, moving away from a mere 'performance' or the identity of the 'saviour'. It is the refusal to abuse the underprivileged to build up a positive image of self in research and education.
Epistemic responsibility: Moral accountability to open up to a diversity of thoughts in relation to interculturality, to be curious about other ways of thinking and speaking about the notion.
Far-but-close: This somewhat contradictory adjective refers to the importance of taking into account both distance and closeness in the way we engage with ideas, ideologies, words, concepts, notions, methods, scholars ... in relation to interculturality. A position which is considered to be not too close, not too distant – *balanced*.
Fieldcentrism: Refers to the tendency to make use of and refer to (dominating) knowledge produced exclusively in a (sub-)field of research related to interculturality, ignoring discussions of the same topic/issue in other fields, other languages and other times.
Fogainsting: Portmanteau verb combining the adverbs *for* and *against*, indicating that one might not hold a clear-cut position about a specific issue (not for, not against but both).
Huiwen (回文词): Type of Chinese poem that is palindromic, reversible, and circular without any (obvious) end or beginning but *infinite ends and beginnings*. *Hui* means *back, to return, to revolve, to curve, to cycle*. Picking a word from the poem randomly one can 'start' a new poem by navigating randomly through the words around it. As a metaphor for interculturality, it reminds us that the notion should be treated unsystematically and purposelessly, exploring her multiple entry points.
Ideological aerophagia: An uncritical position concerning interculturality as a result of 'swallowing too much air', i.e. taking for granted what a scholar or a decision-maker claims about the notion without questioning the content of their assertions.

Appendix: List of terms proposed by the author

Ideological clash: Since interculturality is examined, discussed and dealt with through an uncountable number of ideological positions around the world and within specific economic-political spaces, when people negotiate e.g. the definition or implementation of interculturality, their disagreements (guided by what can only be described as 'narrow' ideological positions) lead them to clashes. Often, one might camouflage such quarrels under the guise of 'culture clash' or 'intercultural misunderstanding', brushing aside the influence of economic/political elements.

Ideological cocoon: Wrapping oneself in one's certainties and ideological universe, following specific 'orders'. Protecting oneself from other ideologies, closing the door to external influences in the way we deal with interculturality in research and education.

Ideological drills: Perfecting one's certitude about interculturality by rehearsing specific ideologies while rejecting others.

Ideological inbreeding: As a member of a given academic tribe or a teaching team, interacting, feeding on and cooperating exclusively with scholars or teachers who share one's ideologies of interculturality.

Ideological injustice: Purposefully ignoring, negating, discarding ideologies of interculturality perceived to be 'inferior', 'inoperative' or 'not worthy of contemplation'.

Ideological mimetism: Mimicking an ideological stance towards interculturality to e.g. get published or access to a research group. Mimetism can also occur when one does not have access to alternative models or ideologies for interculturality.

Ideological mis-drawering: Neologism referring to misplacing a scholar, an idea, a concept into an ideological category that does not match their original position.

Ideological occultation: Hiding alternative ideologies of interculturality from view on purpose or because of one's ignorance of what they represent and/or entail.

Intellectual 'clutches': (see ideological drills)

Interculturality as *je ne sais quoi*: French for *I know not what*. Since interculturality is a polysemous, highly complex and unstable notion in global research and education, always dependent on specific economic-political positions, she cannot be adequately described or expressed.

Interculturality-as-a-zombie: Refers to a form of interculturality that is contained in empty, meaningless and automatic discourses. Interculturality lacking substance.

Interculturality-as-change: A tautology used to emphasise the centrality of change and transformation in interculturality as a subject of research and education. Interculturality as a word already indicates change but, by adding *as-change*, one hopes to bring attention to this vital aspect of the notion.

Interculturalising interculturality-*ism*: I have proposed and developed with Jacobsson (Dervin, 2021; Dervin & Jacobsson, 2022) the idea of interculturalising interculturality – making interculturality a notion that is treated in complex ways, interculturalising it. This entry refers to the potential impossibility to achieve interculturalising since one's take on interculturality cannot but be influenced and limited by the language that we use and our ignorance of the thousands of different ways of conceptualising interculturality around the world. *Who interculturalises what?* and *who is entitled to interculturalise and for whom?* are important questions to consider when tackling this issue.

Interculturalspeak-phobia: The dislike, fear and/or disapproval of (what might appear as) certain automatic and uncritical ways of speaking about interculturality.

Interculturating: Neologism used by one of my Chinese students – was it a slip of the tongue? – to turn interculturality into a verb, indicating an action, a potentially never-ending process. Action of 'doing' interculturality.

Interculturologies: Portmanteau word based on interculturality and mythologies. Interculturologies correspond to the study of imagined forms and myths of interculturality.

Kinetophilia: Term one could use to refer to the necessity to 'love and appreciate movement and mobility' in the way we think about interculturality as a subject of research and education.

Non-essentialism as a gimmick: Use of the popularity of and the somewhat sense of invisibility that non-essentialism can provide us with to manipulate others into thinking that what they do is objectionable. At the same time, this allows the one using non-essentialism as a gimmick to construct a self-image blown out of proportion ('superman') – *I do not essentialise*.

Pantomime: From Latin (*pantomimus*) for *imitators of everything*, a pantomime is someone who tries different things, imitates them, without thinking too much about the ethical consequences of adopting e.g. ideologies that might not be compatible with the local 'orders' that are preferred in their own context. Pantomimes of interculturality imitate everything without thinking.

Pantonality: In music, treats different tones on an equal footing. Helps us call for scholars, educators and decision-makers to consider different ways of problematising and dealing with interculturality equally.

Peau de Chagrin: From a novel by Balzac (1831/2012), in which the main character buys a magical Chagrin skin (a wild ass's skin) which can fulfil any wish. He dies when the skin has shrunk after each wish was accomplished. Reminds us that 'miraculous' solutions to our wishes about interculturality ('models', 'theoretical stances disguised under the political', 'magical concepts') cannot but be illusionary, short-lived and filled with unexpected consequences.

Procrustean thinking: Considering interculturality from a limited, one-sided and biased angle, ignoring the potential input of less prized perspectives, methods and ideologies.

Shelf impact: In business, refers to the popularity and success of a product placed in strategic places on shelves and gondolas – for which companies pay a premium. Research on interculturality is also based on the principle of 'shelf impact'. Being influential in the field often seems to have to do with specific geo-economic-political positions (the 'West', English-speaking, top institutions, consultancy for powerful supranational institutions).

Sloganism: Argument, idea, opinion and/or stand about interculturality expressed and uttered as a mantra, motto, catchphrase in research and education.

Terrae incognitae: Latin for unexplored countries or fields of knowledge. Refers here to unknown strands of intercultural knowledge from outside the 'centre', the 'West'. These could include (amongst others): *Agonistic Palabre* (African procedure), *Community of Shared Future* (China), *Dowa education* (Japan), *Inter- culturalidad* (South America), *Interculturalité* (some French-speaking countries), *Ubuntu* (South Africa) (see Dervin & Jacobsson, 2022, p. 14).

References

Balzac, H. de (1831/2012). *The Wild Ass's Skin*. Oxford: OUP.

Dervin, F. (2021). Critical and reflexive languaging in the construction of interculturality as an object of research and practice (19 April 2021). *Digital series of talks on plurilingualism and interculturality*, University of Copenhagen.

Dervin, F. & Jacobsson, A. (2022). *Intercultural Communication Education. Broken Realities and Rebellious Dreams*. London: Springer.

Index

Achilles' heels 15, 48
alienation 8, 16, 68
alternative knowledge 14, 24, 26, 31, 38, 45, 48, 53, 115
Atelophilia 56, 126

Beckett, S. 1–2, 4, 124
bias 13, 16, 22, 86, 98, 106, 130
binary 22

cage 4, 9, 49–50, 121
capitalism 50, 92, 102
change 8–9, 11, 15, 29, 34–36, 39–40, 45, 50, 53, 60–61, 68, 75–76, 80, 99, 101, 103–106, 113–114, 119, 12, 128–129
China 2, 10, 13, 24, 26, 39–41, 52, 68, 70, 73, 86, 92, 105, 116, 130
citizenship 10, 23–24, 29, 44, 58, 61, 63, 87, 112, 118
cocoon 69, 108, 119, 128
contradiction 3, 7, 13, 16, 69, 71, 76, 78, 80, 94, 98, 101, 103–104, 122, 126
criticality 10–11, 14, 15–16, 43, 46, 82, 84–88, 95–96, 106, 122–123, 126–127
criticality of criticality 15–16, 43, 46, 86, 88, 95, 123, 126
criticentrism 86–127

decolonising 6, 12, 14–15, 24, 26–27, 39, 52, 55, 58–60, 83, 85–87, 91, 122
democracy 23–24, 27, 44, 58, 61, 80, 91–92, 122

dialogue 7, 9, 13, 24, 28, 36, 39, 68, 80, 93, 94, 110, 122, 124
differilitude 75, 112
dominating voices 110
doxa 3, 14, 21, 33, 35, 41, 50, 110, 122

emancipate 14, 41–42, 45
English 12, 13, 27, 35, 40–42, 51, 61, 80–81, 84, 85, 88, 93, 95, 98, 109, 116, 118, 130
epistemologies 5, 7, 14, 15, 27
essentialism 34, 38–39, 56
ethics 71, 106
etymology 3, 8, 12, 74, 81, 103, 106, 110, 118
Europe 4, 14, 21, 23–24, 26–27, 30, 36–37, 41, 47, 50–52, 54, 61, 70, 87, 93, 102, 110, 117

faces 54, 89, 105, 111, 126
failure 33, 60, 62
Finland 3, 5, 13, 30, 102
fragments 7, 10–16, 21, 72, 121, 122–124

ghosts 26, 28, 59
Global South 8, 25, 40, 42, 44–45, 60, 63, 81, 88, 95, 99, 115, 122, 127
guru 52, 55, 74, 113

harmony 73, 76, 118
huiwen 76, 127

identity 55, 59, 90, 92, 118, 127
ideological aerophagia 28, 127
ideological clash 42, 46, 54, 128

ideology 3, 8–11, 14–15, 18, 26–29, 32–33, 36–37, 40–47, 49, 52, 77–79, 81, 86–89, 92, 116, 126, 128, 130
injustice 2, 4, 42, 52, 89, 91, 95, 122, 128
intercultural competence 4, 26, 29, 34, 41, 57, 63, 70–71, 92, 110, 120, 122
interculturologies 21, 129

kinetophilia 50, 129

language 4, 8, 10, 12–13, 16, 21, 27–28, 30, 35, 39, 48, 50, 54, 61–62, 69, 72, 81, 87–88, 93–95, 99, 107, 109, 110, 115–116, 118–119, 123, 127, 129
listen to 5, 15, 21, 40, 42, 43, 60, 67, 77–79, 94, 109, 114, 116, 119

mask 40, 42, 77, 87, 110, 111
mimetism 14, 29, 54, 128
Minzu 10, 26, 42–43, 35, 54, 68
mirror 7, 51, 72, 77–78, 91, 94, 98–99, 123, 126
miscommunication 30
model 4, 35, 50, 67, 92, 106, 121, 128, 130
money 5, 22, 25, 32, 35, 52, 59, 62, 91–92, 95
multicultural 2, 10, 23, 28–29, 54, 56–57, 121
multilingual 11, 40, 62, 95, 110
myth 14, 17, 21, 31, 59, 71, 129

nihilism 1, 88, 100
noise 44–46, 72
non-essentialism 15, 21, 22, 24–26, 29, 31, 33–35, 44–45, 57–59, 80, 87, 91, 122, 129

obvious 3–4, 10, 26, 32, 36, 44–45, 67, 105, 116–117, 121, 127
orders 8, 10, 13, 15, 35, 43, 48, 55, 57, 61, 67, 74, 77, 79, 106, 119, 122, 128–129

paradoxes 3, 21
politics 3, 5–6, 25, 54, 88, 91, 110, 112
polysemy 3, 10, 22, 40, 50, 78, 84, 87, 89, 109, 122, 124, 128
portmanteau 99, 112, 127, 129
power 4–5, 10, 14, 24–25, 39, 42, 48, 52, 58–59, 60, 84, 92, 110, 113, 123, 130
procrustean thinking 52, 130
propaganda 25, 41, 59, 88

racism 2, 51, 58, 91, 117
reader 5, 7–16, 27–28, 43, 57, 59, 67, 80, 83, 90, 102, 118–119, 123–124
reflexivity 8, 11, 24, 85, 127
rethink 6–7, 16, 38, 45–46, 77, 90, 96, 98–103, 106, 121, 123
ritornellos 33, 44, 46, 122

shelf impact 91, 130
silence 1, 4, 5, 38, 87, 114, 122
slogan 15, 28, 34, 48, 51, 130
stereotype 13–14, 21, 25, 33, 35, 45, 61, 73, 80, 86

taken-for-granted 4, 104
terrae incognitae 45, 130
transcultural 40, 81, 121
translanguaging 26
translation 6, 11, 21, 33, 42, 54, 86, 103, 109, 116

unfaithful 108, 118, 122, 123
unstable 6, 9, 21, 33, 54, 98, 109, 111, 123–124, 128
unthink 7, 16, 39, 46, 96, 98–101, 103, 106, 121, 123

voices 5, 14, 25, 28, 38, 44, 49, 59, 62, 72, 79–80, 87, 109–110, 122

whiteness 16, 24, 42, 51–52, 55, 99, 127

zombie 111–128

For Product Safety Concerns and Information please contact our EU
representative GPSR@taylorandfrancis.com
Taylor & Francis Verlag GmbH, Kaufingerstraße 24, 80331 München, Germany

www.ingramcontent.com/pod-product-compliance
Lightning Source LLC
Chambersburg PA
CBHW070554170426
43201CB00012B/1836